Definitive Guide to sed

Tutorial and Reference

Definitive Guide to sed

Tutorial and Reference

by Daniel A. Goldman

EHDP Press

Definitive Guide to sed

Tutorial and Reference

ISBN: 978-1-939824-02-8 (Print version)
02248803331822
EHDP Press
http://www.sed-book.com/

Copyright (c) 2013 Daniel A. Goldman. All rights reserved. No part of this book may be reproduced, stored in a retrieval system, or transmitted, without prior written permission of the author. While great care has been taken in the preparation of this book, the author assumes no responsibility for errors or omissions, or for damages resulting from the use of the information in this book.

This version has the same content as the separate Kindle and EPUB versions of the book. The formatting has been optimized for print display, using the LaTeX documentation preparation system.

The cover shows an example of how sed ('stream editor') works. In the example, input comes from a text file. Using instructions from a 'sed script' that you write, sed edits the input text, line by line, to produce modified output.

The sed script: 1) changes the word 'Input' to 'Output'; 2) changes 'sed' to 'SED' (but only if 'sed' occurs at the beginning of a line); and 3) changes 'a' to 'my' (but only if 'a' is a complete word). This gives an inkling of the power and flexibility of sed, as fully explained in this book.

Table of Contents

Foreword xi

Preface xii

1: Introduction to sed 1

    sed is a 'Stream Editor' 1
    PatSpace and HoldSpace 3
    Introducing the s Command 4
    Quoting Command-Line Scripts 5
    Inputs used in Book Examples 6

2: sed s Command (substitute) 9

    Delimiter for s Command 9
    sed Input from File or stdin 10
    sed Command Line Options 12
    -e sed Command Line Option 12
    ; sed Command Line Syntax 13
    -f sed Command Line Option 14
    sed Output to File or stdout 15
    -i sed Command Line Option 17

3: Flags for s (substitute) Command 19

    i (ignore case) Flag 20
    g (global) and n (number) Flags 21
    -n sed Command Line Option 22
    p (print) and w (write) Flags 23
    e (execute) and m (multi) Flags 25
    Combining s Command Flags 27

4: Single Character MetaChars 29

    Literal Character in RegEx 29
    . (Wildcard Character) 32
    \ (Specify Literal Character) 32
    [ ] (Character Set) 34
    \w \W (Word and Non-Word) 36
    [: :] (Posix Character Class) 38

Contents

5: Anchor MetaChars 42

^ (Start of PatSpace) 42
$ (End of PatSpace) 44
\< \> \b (Word Boundaries) 46
\B (Not a Word Boundary) 49

6: Simple Repetition MetaChars 50

* (0 or More of Previous) 50
\+ (1 or More of Previous) 53
-r sed Command Line Option 53
\? (0 or 1 of Previous) 54
* \+ \? Compared 56

7: General Repetition MetaChars 58

\{N\} (Exact N of Previous) 58
\{L,\} (Low, Higher of Previous) 59
\{L,H\} (Low, High of Previous) 60

8: Other RegEx MetaChars 62

\| (Alternative Patterns) 62
\(\) (Grouping and Saving) 63
\` (Always Start of PatSpace) 65
\' (Always End of PatSpace) 65

9: SubEx MetaChars 67

& (Entire Matched Portion) 67
\N BackRef (Play Saved Group) 68
\l \u (Case for Next Character) 70
\L \U \E (Case for Next Span) 71

10: Command Addresses 73

Address Omitted 74
N Format Address 74
L,H Format Address 75
/RegEx/ Format Address 76
/RegEx/,/RegEx/ Address 78
L,/RegEx/ Format Address 79
/RegEx/,+N Format Address 81
/RegEx/,~N Format Address 82
First~Step Address 83
! (Inverts Address Match) 84

11: Delete PatSpace Content - dD 86

sed d Command (delete) 86
sed D Command (Delete) 89

Contents

12: Append, Insert, Change - aic **90**

    sed a Command (append) 90
    sed i Command (insert) 91
    sed c Command (change) 92
    aic Syntax Alternatives 93
    Cannot Edit a, i, c Results 95

13: Print PatSpace - pP l **98**

    sed p Command (print) 98
    sed P Command (Print) 99
    sed l Command (display line) 100

14: Read / Write File - rR wW **101**

    sed r Command (read Rfile) 102
    sed R Command (Read Rfile) 103
    sed w Command (write Wfile) 105
    sed W Command (Write Wfile) 107

15: Read Line into PatSpace - nN **109**

    sed n Command (next line) 109
    sed N Command (Next Line) 111

16: Access HoldSpace - hH gG x **112**

    sed h Command (hold) 113
    sed H Command (Hold) 113
    sed g Command (get) 113
    sed G Command (Get) 113
    sed x Command (exchange) 113
    Examples - HoldSpace (gGhHx) 114

17: Branch / Quit - : btT / qQ **116**

    sed : (Label, eg :k) 116
    sed b Command (branch) 116
    sed t Command (test) 117
    sed T Command (Test) 117
    Branching Examples 117
    sed q Command (quit) 119
    sed Q Command (Quit) 120

18: Other Actions - { } #eyvz = ... **121**

    sed { } (grouping) 121
    sed #(comment marker) 123
    sed e Command (execute) 124
    sed v Command (version) 124
    sed y Command (transliterate) 124

Contents

  sed z Command (zap) 125
  sed = Command (line #) 125

19: General Advice about sed 127

  When to Use (or not Use) sed 127
  Quoting Command-Line Scripts 128
  Using sed within Shell Scripts 130
  Testing sed Scripts 131
  Structuring Input Files 131

20: Examples - Substitution 134

  Do a Simple Substitution 134
  Substitute for a Span 134
  Add Leader at Line Start 135
  Delete Space at Line Start 135
  Delete Space at Line End 135
  Substitute only for a Word 136
  Substitute for One or More (+) 136
  Substitute up to Something 136
  Substitute on Certain Lines 137
  Replace with Entire Match 137
  Replace All or Just One 137

21: Examples - Line Spacing 138

  Double Space a Stream 138
  Triple Space a Stream 139
  Squeeze Blank Lines to One 140

22: Examples - Add Some Lines 142

  Add Line Before Lines 1, 3, ... 142
  Add Line After Lines 2, 3, ... 142
  Add Line Before Matching Line 143
  Add Line After Matching Line 144
  Add Line Before & After Line 145

23: Examples - Print Some Lines 146

  Print Line #X 146
  Print Last Line 146
  Print Lines L to H 147
  Print First X Lines 147
  Print Last X Lines 148
  Print Lines 4, 8, ... 149
  Print Matching Line 149
  Print Line Before Match 149
  Print Line After Match 150
  Number Lines in Stream 151

Contents

24: Examples - Delete Some Lines **152**

    Delete Line #X 152
    Delete Last Line 153
    Delete Lines L to H 153
    Delete First X Lines 153
    Delete Last X Lines 154
    Delete Lines 1, 3, ... 154
    Delete All Blank Lines 155
    Delete Leading Blank Lines 156
    Delete Up to Blank Line #1 156
    Delete Match-Based Range 157
    Delete Following Matched Line 157
    Delete Serial Duplicate Lines 158

25: Examples - Other Short Tasks **160**

    Count Lines in Stream 160
    Delete Duplicate Characters 161
    Format a Phone Number 161
    Capitalize Words 161
    Replace First Match in File 162
    Reverse Each Word 162
    Reverse Each Line 163
    Reverse Order of Lines 164
    Add Commas to Numbers 165

26: Examples - Complex Tasks **166**

    Add Headers and Footers 166
    Multi-Line Find and Replace 170
    Set Incremental Macro Values 174
    Delete HTML Tags 178

27: Related Unix Commands - grep **182**

    grep Usage 182
    grep Command Line Options 184

28: Other Related Commands - 1/2 . . . . **195**

    head - Print First Part of File 195
    tail - Print Last Part of File 197
    uniq - Handle Repeated Lines 200
    tr - Translate Characters 203

29: Other Related Commands - 2/2 . . . . **206**

    expr - Evaluate an Expression 207
    seq - Print Number Sequence 209

Contents

30: Definitions of Special Terms 212

31: sed Command Line Reference 214

32: sed Command Reference 220

33: s Command Flag Reference 229

34: Address and RegEx Reference 233

35: Related Books and Web Sites 242

Concepts Index 245

Command / Syntax Index 248

Script Examples Index 252

Foreword

A few months ago, I got a request from the author, Daniel Goldman, to write the foreword for this book. I have written lots of software. I have maintained GNU sed for many years, along with other open source projects. But I had never written a foreword. So I initially did not quite know what to make of his request.

I have had a chance to communicate with the author over several months. Through all this time, I have enjoyed Daniel's enthusiasm for the project, and I have grown to share it with him. I have come to appreciate his attention to detail and concern for the reader. I hope our discussions helped improve the book, and I am really happy to write this little piece of it.

sed has been around for decades, but it is still a very useful tool. Yet, the distinctly different syntax and operation often makes it tough for beginning users to get the hang of sed.

For this reason, learning resources are very important, and I can recommend this book as a good way to learn and review sed. It will help beginners get up to speed, and at the same time serve as a useful reference for everyone.

I hope that this book is well received. The effort put in by the author, and the high quality of the result, surely deserve that.

Paolo Bonzini
GNU sed maintainer (2004-2012)

Preface

sed is a 'stream editor'. sed lets you rapidly and efficiently edit multiple 'streams' (text files and program outputs). If you process and transform source code, documentation, data, or other text, adding sed to your toolkit will increase your productivity.

This book guides you step-by-step to master sed. I have used sed over 20 years, in combination with other Unix utilities. I would like to share my knowledge of sed with you.

My background using sed:

For many years, sed has been my constant companion to help edit and process source code, documentation, program outputs, and data files.

I write and maintain software. I have used sed to help edit and transform source code files written in several programming languages.

I do a lot of technical writing. sed helps me edit and maintain web sites, help files, and user guides. It even helped write this book.

I write a lot of Unix shell scripts, to automate various tasks. I use sed within shell scripts to help process outputs from commands, and do other transformations.

Finally, I import data into data warehouse software, for analysis. I have used sed to help quickly process and import complex text data files, with millions of records.

What I observed (the need):

Besides sed, I have extensively used other languages and tools: Bash, C, C#, cairo, CSS, DOM, Excel, GD, gettext, HTML, ICD coding, Java, JavaScript, Linux, SQL, vi, various others.

For these technologies, I found it possible to understand any feature or option I needed.

In contrast, although I was using sed frequently, much of sed remained a mystery to me. I found sed to be a useful way to process text, but my efforts to master sed proved disappointing.

I found relatively few books and tutorials on sed. And those few resources seemed incomplete and not well enough written. Other people reported similar feelings. They liked sed, but found it confusing to learn.

What I decided to do:

It seemed a shame sed lacked a first-rate book, an easy and complete way to learn sed. I felt I had the needed range of technical and writing skills to fill the gap. So I decided to write this book.

I went back to the basics. I pored through the GNU sed man page and manual, and other available information sources, to refresh my knowledge of sed, and clarify any uncertainties.

Then, I put that knowledge into a format and wording that others can easily learn from. I made up simple examples to cover every aspect of sed, and to show how sed cooperates with other Unix utilities.

Overall, it took more than a year of effort. The result is this book, the sed book 'I wish I had when I learned'.

Style of this book:

I believe the best way to learn sed is to use it. Theory has its place, but there is no substitute for hands-on use. So I have provided hundreds of examples, to make this a practical book.

I have avoided obscure or complex examples as much as possible. As explained more in Chapter 19, I think the real strength of sed is in doing simple operations, often in combination with other Unix utilities. So I have focused on simple, clean usage in this book.

In addition, I think over-detailed and long-winded examples bog readers down. I have read many software books, and become educated in technical writing. I think readers learn better from simple examples.

sed has a unique way of operating. But once you get the hang of it, sed is useful and fun. My goal is to make it much easier for you to reach that comfort level, and provide a ready reference for any time needed in the future.

What this book covers:

This book covers GNU sed, the most popular and arguably the best sed. Version 4.2.1 is covered.

It is beyond the scope of this book, and probably of little general interest, to document the many differences between GNU sed and other seds. It is recommended to use GNU sed, because it is generally better for writing one-line scripts, and allows for cleaner syntax.

If you use a different sed than GNU sed, this book is still useful for learning, since most of the commands are the same. This book indicates the commands that are 'GNU extensions' (specially added to GNU sed).

A lot of the power of sed arises from pattern matching. sed and pattern matching go hand in hand. So this book completely covers sed regular expressions (RegEx), for pattern matching.

Finally, this book also explains and documents the GNU versions of the related (and useful) commands grep, head, tail, uniq, tr, seq, and expr.

Preface

Availability and installation of sed:

sed is part of the base installation for Linux, BSD, Mac OS X, IBM AIX, HP/UX, Solaris, and other Unix-like systems. These are very good environments for using sed, because the Unix shell and Unix utilities will be present.

It is recommended that non-Linux users install GNU sed, because it is generally better for writing one-line scripts. One way is to download and compile the GNU sed source code, but this is a huge bother and normally not needed.

Most Unix versions include GNU sed by default, or have a way to readily install it. For example, FreeBSD includes GNU sed ("gsed") by default, along with the FreeBSD version of sed.

Solaris 11 includes a version of sed. It also installs GNU sed to /usr/bin with the command "pkg install //solaris/text/gnu-sed". Solaris 10 installs GNU sed to /opt/sfw with the command "pkgadd -d SFWsed".

http://hpux.connect.org.uk/hppd/hpux/Gnu/ lets an HP-UX administrator download and install GNU sed to the /usr/local directory. HP-UX has it's own version of sed installed.

IBM AIX comes with a version of sed. Also, the "AIX Toolbox for Linux Applications" may be installed to an IBM AIX computer, and includes GNU sed (as well as other common GNU utilities).

minised and ssed ("super-sed") are two other well-developed sed versions. minised is small and fast. ssed includes Perl regular expressions. If you don't already use one of these, it is suggested to use GNU sed instead.

sed may also be installed to and used on a Windows computer. If you go this route, search for 'GnuWin32 download sed', and follow the instructions on the GNU sed web site.

sed is also included in MKS Toolkit and Cygwin (GNU sed), Unix-like environments that run under Windows.

Who will benefit from this book:

Unix and Linux Users - sed fits in well with the Unix way of doing things. If you are already using Unix, you will benefit from knowing sed.

Software developers - sed can help maintain source code and documentation. In combination with other Unix tools, it is a fast way to make global changes. sed is incredibly more efficient than 'hunt and peck'.

Technical writers - If you edit HTML, LaTeX, DocBook, troff, or other text, sed can help to maintain and process the files. For example, this book was edited and processed with the help of sed.

Web site developers - sed can help edit and process multi-page web sites.

Data users - sed can help edit and import text data files. The author uses sed to import and verify large health-related data files.

Anyone using lots of text - sed can be helpful for editing various other text files, such as log files or whatever else you deal with.

Preface

This book is for those who want to work faster, easier, and more reliably by automating tasks. The book is for those who edit text files, and do not want to be limited to 'point and click' / 'hunt and peck' operations.

sed does not normally edit binary files such as Word documents. sed is designed to work with text files, with each line terminated with a newline.

You are often better off using text files instead of binary files, anyway. Text files are readable by countless editors and utilities, are non-proprietary, are easily shared with anyone, and are guaranteed to be readable in the future.

Prerequisites:

Because sed has Unix roots, and is most often used on Unix, the examples in this book use Unix.

If you plan to use sed on Unix, it is recommended to be familiar with basic Unix commands (eg, cat, cd, chmod, cp, echo, ls, man, mkdir, more, mv, rm, rmdir) and to have written some simple shell scripts.

If you plan to use sed on Windows, it is recommended to be familiar with batch or PowerShell scripting.

This book explains the Unix concepts needed to understand the examples. But it is beyond the scope of this book to serve as a general introduction to Unix. For those new to Unix, Chapter 35 lists Unix-related books and web sites to help you learn.

You can also run most of the examples in this book from a Windows command prompt, and use sed on a Windows PC, assuming you have also installed a set of Unix utilities, such as 'UnxUtils'.

From http://sourceforge.net/projects/unxutils/, download UnxUtils.zip to a new directory (eg, c:\unxutils\), and unzip the file. Then, edit the Windows 'Path' variable (Start | Control Panel | System | Advanced | Environmental Variables) to include 'c:\unxutils\usr\local\wbin\'.

Special Terms:

A clearly defined vocabulary is essential in any technical field. To improve communication of sed-related concepts, this book consistently uses the following short special terms: Address, AutoPrint, BackRef, BackSlash, Cycle, Delimiter, HoldSpace, Literal, MetaChar, PatSpace, RegEx, SubEx, Word, stdin, stdout, and stderr.

Part of the confusion for learning sed is that a variety of terms are used in different books and learning resources. To help clear this up, as much as possible I have used the same terminology as the GNU sed manual. To indicate the special nature of these terms, I capitalize the ones I 'made up'.

Instead of bogging the book down here, each special term is explained the first time it is used in the book. For your convenience, Chapter 30 also defines all the special terms.

Preface

Chapters in this book:

    How sed Works / s Command - Chapters 1-3 cover how sed edits a text stream, sample inputs used within this book, and the s (substitute) command that 'finds and replaces'.
    MetaChar / RegEx / SubEx - Chapters 4-9 explain how to do pattern matching in sed: metacharacters (MetaChar), regular expressions (RegEx) and substitution expressions (SubEx).
    sed Command Line Options - Each main command line option, such as -r, is covered separately in the book location where it first makes sense. This makes the book flow better.
    sed Addresses - Chapter 10 explains 'Addresses', such as '1' in '1d'. The Address determines when a sed command runs.
    Other sed Commands - Chapters 11-18 explain the remaining 25 or so sed commands (beside the s command), with many examples.
    General Advice - Chapter 19 gives general information and advice about using sed.
    sed Examples - Chapters 20-26 show and explain task-oriented examples of using sed. Working through the examples will increase your understanding.
    Related Commands - Chapters 27-29 explain useful GNU Linux commands related to sed (grep, head, tail, uniq, tr, seq, and expr) with examples.
    Special Terms - Each special term, such as 'PatSpace', is explained in the text the first time used. Chapter 30 gathers together all the explanations.
    Reference - Chapters 30-34 summarize sed command line options, sed commands, sed flags, and sed regular expressions.

    This book presents sed information in two different ways: Tutorial and Reference. You can read each of these 'books' independently of the others. The content is the same.
    The **Tutorial** (Chapters 1-18) explains each concept in detail, with many examples. The **Reference** (Chapters 30-34) summarizes each concept.
    In addition, Chapters 20-26 present and explain sed examples, and Chapters 27-29 explain related Unix commands, such as grep and uniq.
    Learning all of sed can be a daunting task. This book is ordered in importance and usefulness of the topics: 1) s (substitute) command; 2) regular expresssions (RegEx); 3) command Addresses; 4) other commands (besides s).
    If you have any corrections, suggestions, comments or questions related to this book, please contact the author on the http://www.sed-book.com/ web site.

Preface

Acknowledgments:

All content of this book is solely the responsibility of the author. However, I am grateful to all who have developed, documented, and supported sed. Here are a few key individuals:

Al Aab, Arnold Robbins, Aurelio Jargas, Bruce Barnett, Dale Dougherty, Eric Pement, Greg Ubben, Jay Fenlason, Ken Pizzini, Lee McMahon, Paolo Bonzini, Sven Guckes, Yao-Jen Chang. I apologize if I have left anyone off.

Many of the scripts in this book have been used or modified from those presented by Eric Pement, Paolo Bonzini, Peteris Krumins, and Yao-Jen Chang.

I thank Paolo Bonzini, for his open mindedness and good nature, his helpful suggestions, and for all the time and energy he spent maintaining GNU sed.

I also thank Sven Guckes, for his many years running the sed-users Yahoo group, and his helpful comments on this book.

Summary of information:

What are the advantages of sed?

- It is very useful for processing text files.
- It has full regular expression capabilities.
- It is compact, with a limited command set.
- You can master sed (with this book's help).

What are barriers to learning sed?

- sed has a unique way of doing things.
- You cannot learn sed from man pages.
- Other learning resources are inadequate.

What is special about this book?

- Includes hundreds of real examples.
- Covers all features of GNU sed.
- Includes full tutorial and reference.

Why is this book useful for you?

- Is the best and fastest way to learn sed.
- Saves you many hours now and later.
- Lets you work much more efficiently.

1: Introduction to sed

This chapter introduces sed:

1) How sed edits files and program outputs.
2) PatSpace and HoldSpace work areas.
3) Basics of finding and replacing.
4) Basics of quoting sed scripts.

sed is a 'Stream Editor'

'sed' is a 'stream editor', a special kind of text editor. sed is a fast and efficient way of editing multiple text files (or editing program outputs).

Referring back to the example on the book cover: Using instructions from a 'sed script' that you write, sed edits input text, line by line, to produce modified output.

———

vi, emacs, and other 'text editors' (NotePad++, TextMate, etc.) are powerful. But they are slow and cumbersome for making repetitive edits to large numbers of files.

sed cannot substitute for a text editor, such as vi or emacs. And a text editor cannot substitute for sed. They are fundamentally different technologies. Here are some differences:

1) vi and emacs edit a text file on disk. In contrast, sed edits a text 'stream' (read from a file, or read from another program).

2) vi and emacs receive manual instructions from keyboard and mouse. sed runs automatically, based on a 'sed script' you have written.

3) vi and emacs jump to any position in a file. sed reads input one line at a time, from first line to last line, and applies edits to each line.

———

The very successful **Unix philosophy** uses the shell and small Unix utilities, connected with pipes or intermediate files, as opposed to using large monolithic programs.

As expressed by Kernighan and Pike, Unix created 'a new style of computing, a new way of thinking of how to attack a problem with a computer. This style was based on the use of tools: using programs separately or in combination to get a

Chapter 1

job done, rather than doing it by hand, by monolithic self-sufficient subsystems, or by special-purpose, one-time programs'.

Used appropriately (Chapter 19), sed fits in well with the Unix philosophy. sed coexists happily with text files, shell scripts, pipes, filters, and other Unix utilities.

For example, sed input can come from another program, and sed output can be sent to another program:

```
$ prg_1 | sed 's/A/B/' | prg_2
$ cut -c 9 file | sed s/A/B/ | sort
$ grep =3= file | sed s/A/B/ | head
```

For those new to Unix, '$' is the Unix command prompt, and '|' is the pipe that connects output from prg_1 to input for sed, and connects sed output to input for prg_2. Two examples of 'prg_1' and 'prg_2' are shown in the box above.

Alternatives to sed: awk and perl can also do 'stream editing', and are both quite useful. However, my experience has led me to prefer sed for many tasks. Here are some differences:

awk is really designed as a report writer, works best with input fields and records, and is more complex than sed. In contrast, sed is designed as a more general-purpose stream editor, and has no notion of input fields.

Both sed and awk read and process an input file one line at a time. So there is a fundamental similarity.

However, there are a huge number of differences in syntax and function. So it would likely be very confusing learning sed and awk at the same time. I would recommend getting comfortable with one (or the other) first, and then it will be easier to pick up the other one.

perl is a general-purpose programming language. It will do just about any kind of scripting task. But it is quite complex, even more complex than awk.

sed is an efficient and compact way to rapidly edit text files and program outputs. With the help of this book, you can master sed, and learn to use it in a way that is clean and maintainable.

Very brief history: sed is a very early Unix command, created soon after the breakthrough grep utility. sed was originally developed by Lee McMahon at Bell Labs, from 1973 to 1974. Later, other contributors wrote new versions of sed, and sed became integrated into GNU software.

sed is largely based on the 'ed' editor (written by Ken Thompson), present on virtually every Unix computer.

ed is a primitive kind of editor. For example, it views only one line at a time! It is a relic from the days of slow connections and teletype consoles.

On the positive side, ed includes powerful commands and regular expressions. Elements of ed have influenced awk, ex, grep, perl, sed, vi, and other tools.

Because of the shared elements, if you learn one of these technologies (such as sed), learning another (such as grep or vi) will be much easier.

PatSpace and HoldSpace

sed is a text processing utility with its own scripting language. sed is **not** a general-purpose programming language. For example, sed lacks variables and arrays.

However, sed does have two special 'buffers' or 'work spaces'. Throughout the book, to clearly identify them and for brevity, we call the buffers 'PatSpace' and 'HoldSpace'. To learn sed, you need to understand PatSpace and HoldSpace.

PatSpace (pattern space) is the primary work space used by sed. Most sed operations read or modify PatSpace.

Line by line, sed reads input text into PatSpace. Each time a line is read, it starts a 'Cycle', a sequence of operations to process the line.

sed maintains a 'line counter', which starts at 1 (first line), and is incremented each time an input line is read at the start of a Cycle. The sed n and N commands (Chapter 15) also increment the line counter.

For each line (now in PatSpace), sed carries out commands, as specified by a 'sed script'. Most useful sed scripts are short, but a sed script can be as long as needed.

Finally, when no more commands (end of sed script), sed normally 'AutoPrints' (automatically prints) PatSpace. Then, sed reads the next line into PatSpace, and starts a new Cycle.

HoldSpace (hold space) is the secondary work space used by sed. A few sed commands copy text back and forth between PatSpace and HoldSpace.

HoldSpace is **not** cleared between Cycles, and can be used to accumulate lines. In contrast, PatSpace is usually cleared between Cycles.

For routine uses, HoldSpace is not needed. HoldSpace is used for more complex tasks. HoldSpace adds power, but can be confusing.

You can decide for yourself how much to use HoldSpace. If you end up not using HoldSpace yourself, this book will at least let you understand any sed script that does use HoldSpace.

Enough background. In the next section, we will show sed in practice. The best way to learn sed is through practical applications, as we do for the remainder of this book.

Chapter 1

Introducing the s Command

s (substitute) is by far the most commonly used (and most powerful) sed command. If you only learned one sed command, it would be the s command. So it is a good idea to focus on and learn the s command first.

s basically 'finds and replaces'. It substitutes one thing for another.

Suppose the file 'old.txt' contains the single word 'old'. Here is a simple sed command that changes 'old' to 'new':

```
$ sed 's/old/new/' old.txt
new
```

sed reads 'old' from the file, changes 'old' to 'new', and prints the result. In more detail, here are the steps in this sed Cycle.

- sed reads 'old' into PatSpace.
- Trailing newline is removed.
- s runs, changing 'old' to 'new'.
- sed adds back trailing newline.
- sed 'AutoPrints' PatSpace ('new').
- No more input. So sed exits.

's/RegEx/SubEx/' is the basic syntax for s:

RegEx means 'regular expression', the pattern sed finds. A RegEx can be simple, such as 'old'. Chapters 4-8 explain how to make more flexible RegEx patterns, using 'MetaChars' (metacharacters) to do pattern matching.

SubEx means 'substitution expression', the pattern sed replaces with. A SubEx can be simple, such as 'new'. Chapter 9 explains special MetaChars to use within a SubEx, to make it more flexible.

s tries to find the RegEx (eg, 'old') in PatSpace (eg, 'old'). If it finds a match, the **first matching portion** of PatSpace is changed to SubEx (eg, 'new').

If the RegEx ('red' in the example below) is **not** found, s does nothing, and PatSpace ('old') is not changed, so 'old' AutoPrints at the end of the Cycle:

```
$ sed 's/red/blue/' old.txt
old
```

Quoting Command-Line Scripts

In the following example, 's/old/new/' is called the 'sed script':

```
$ sed 's/old/new/' old.txt
new
```

The 'sed script' is the commands sed carries out. The 's/old/new/' script has one command (find 'old' and replace with 'new').

There are three different ways command-line sed scripts may be quoted:

```
1)   quotes omitted
2)  "double quotes"
3)  'single quotes'
```

For many sed scripts, it does not matter which way you quote the script. For example, the following sed commands behave exactly the same (change 'old' to 'new'):

```
1) sed   s/old/new/   old.txt
2) sed  "s/old/new/"  old.txt
3) sed  's/old/new/'  old.txt
```

If unsure, use 'single quotes'. This book mostly uses 'single quotes', but sometimes omits quotes for brevity. Later in the book (Chapter 19), shell quoting is explained in detail. At this point, those details would just bog us down.

However, before continuing our discussion of the s command, we do need to take a brief detour. We must explain the example inputs used to illustrate the s command and other sed commands.

Chapter 1

Inputs used in Book Examples

To make this book practical, many examples are included. Each example uses input from a defined source, so you can run the commands yourself.

This section defines the inputs, and shows examples of how sed uses them. For now, you do not need to understand how the sed commands work. Just concentrate on the input sources.

The book examples use the 'cat', 'echo', and 'seq' commands (and of course 'sed'), all normally installed on any Unix computer.

If you are using a Windows PC, it is relatively easy to download and unzip a set of Unix utilities to your PC and still run most of the examples.

From http://unxutils.sourceforge.net/, download UnxUtils.zip to a new directory (eg, c:\unxutils\), and unzip the file. Then, edit the Windows PATH variable (Start | Control Panel | System | Advanced | Environmental Variables) to include 'c:\unxutils\usr\local\wbin\'.

http://gnuwin32.sourceforge.net/packages/sed.htm has a recent version of sed for Windows, for you to download. UnxUtils had the older 3.0.2 version when this book was published.

Input #1 is the 'rgb' file. You can create this file using any text editor (eg, vi, emacs, notepad). The Unix 'cat' command displays the two lines in 'rgb':

```
$ cat rgb
lower (#1): "red green blue"
UPPER (#2): "RED GREEN BLUE"
```

Here is an example using the 'rgb' file, to change RED to '123'.

```
$ sed 's/RED/123/' rgb
lower (#1): "red green blue"
UPPER (#2): "123 GREEN BLUE"
```

Introduction to sed

Input #2 - The Unix 'echo' command displays text, which is then used as input for sed. The 'echo -e' command can include newlines (coded as \n):

```
$ echo old
old
$ echo -e "\nold"

old
```

Here is an example using echo, to change 'old' to 'new'. Output from echo is "piped" (|) into sed. You can enter the following command at a Unix prompt:

```
$ echo old | sed 's/old/new/'
new
```

Input #3 - The Unix 'seq' command prints a sequence of numbers, one to a line:

```
$ seq 3
1
2
3
```

Here is an example using seq, to delete line #2. Output from seq is piped into sed:

```
$ seq 3 | sed '2d'
1
3
```

Chapter 1

If seq cannot be installed, you can enter the numbers into a text file (eg, 1-3.txt), and take the input from the file instead of from seq:

```
$ sed '2d' 1-3.txt
1
3
```

Finally, input #4 is the a-i.txt file, with nine lines, one letter per line (a to i). Here is an example using a-i.txt, to delete from the line matching 'a' to the line matching 'g':

```
$ sed '/a/,/g/ d' a-i.txt
h
i
```

Now that we have introduced the example inputs, the next chapter continues discussion of the key s command.

2: sed s Command (substitute)

This chapter is the second of three concerning the s (substitute) command. To review the simplest s command syntax, from the previous chapter:

's/RegEx/SubEx/' searches for RegEx in PatSpace, and replaces ('substitutes') the first matching portion of PatSpace with SubEx. The s command 'finds and replaces'.

RegEx and SubEx can use special 'MetaChars', explained in Chapters 4-9, but for now we just use simple forms like 'old' and 'new'.

Delimiter for s Command

In the 's/RegEx/SubEx/' syntax, '/' is called the 'Delimiter'. It delimits (separates) the different parts of the s command.

Any visible character may be used as the Delimiter. Although '/' is usually used, you may use a different Delimiter.

In practice, only a few alternative Delimiter characters are commonly used, as in the examples below. Of course, do not use something like '3' as the Delimiter. The following examples produce the same result (change 'old' to 'new'):

```
$ echo old | sed 's/old/new/'
$ echo old | sed 's:old:new:'
$ echo old | sed 's|old|new|'
$ echo old | sed 's_old_new_'
```

Chapter 2

If the Delimiter character occurs within the RegEx, you must prefix the character with '\' (BackSlash). '\' tells sed which is which (Delimiter or Literal character). Here is an example to show this:

```
$ echo /A/ | sed 's/\/A\//\/B\//'
/B/
```

'\/' is the Literal 'slash' character. The '\' (BackSlash) tells sed to **not** treat '/' as the Delimiter. '/' (no BackSlash) is the Delimiter. The overall effect is to change '/A/' to '/B/'.

's/\/A\//\/B\//' is called 'Leaning Toothpick' style. Not very pretty, is it? You can get a headache looking at this kind of syntax. To avoid 'Leaning Toothpick', use a different Delimiter. Here is a much better way to write the previous command:

```
$ echo /A/ | sed 's:/A/:/B/:'
/B/
```

Since now the Delimiter is ':' (not '/'), no need to use the '\' BackSlashes. The format is much clearer. Avoid using '\', unless you have to, such as '\n' (newline), '\t' (tab), etc.

Finally, always use three Delimiters, as in 's/A/B/'. 's/A/B' is a common mistake. sed will print an error message if you omit the trailing Delimiter.

sed Input from File or stdin

sed often edits input from a file. Here is an example showing input from the previously defined 'rgb' file:

```
$ sed 's/RED/xxx/' rgb
lower (#1): "red green blue"
UPPER (#2): "xxx GREEN BLUE"
```

sed opens 'rgb', reads the two lines from the file, changes 'RED' to 'xxx', and prints the results to 'stdout' (your computer screen).

sed s Command (substitute)

sed can also read input from 'stdin' (standard input). stdin is either from your keyboard, or from another program, via a '|' pipe.

In practice, sed input almost never comes from the keyboard. But you can do it. For example, enter the command 'sed s/old/new/'. sed will wait for input.

Type xxx and press the Enter key (Return key on some computers). sed prints xxx in reply. Type old and press Enter. sed prints new in reply. Use Ctrl-D (hold down Ctrl key, then press D) to tell sed you are done (end of input).

---

sed input can also come from another command. In the example below, 'echo' sends its output to a '|' pipe. Then, sed reads its input from the pipe:

```
$ echo old | sed 's/old/new/'
new
```

sed reads the line (old), changes 'old' to 'new', and prints the result (new) to stdout.

With few exceptions (eg, -i option), sed operates the same, no matter where the input comes from. So the following inputs (from file and stdin, respectively) produce the same result:

```
$ sed 's/BLUE/xxxx/' rgb
lower (#1): "red green blue"
UPPER (#2): "RED GREEN xxxx"
```

```
$ sed 's/BLUE/xxxx/' < rgb
lower (#1): "red green blue"
UPPER (#2): "RED GREEN xxxx"
```

In the second case, sed receives input from the rgb file, but does not 'know' (or 'care') where the input comes from. The '<' redirects stdin to come from the rgb file.

11

Chapter 2

sed Command Line Options

Almost every Unix command takes 'command line options'. For example, 'ls' (ell ess) lists the directory contents in a basic way, and 'ls -l' produces a 'long listing'.

Unix commands can take a large number of options. For example, 'ls' has some 58 options! sed takes some 12 options, only 5 of which are normally used.

Two commonly used sed options are -e script (add 'script' to end of overall sed script) and -f script-file (add lines in script-file to end of overall script). -e and -f are covered in the next sections.

Other commonly used sed command line options are -i (edit input file 'in place'), -n (suppress AutoPrint of PatSpace), and -r (use extended regular expressions).

We cannot put the cart before the horse and try to explain these other command line options here. Later in the book, each option is explained in the context where it is used.

Chapter 31 lists all the sed command line options, as a convenient reference for you.

-e sed Command Line Option

The 'sed script' is the list of commands that sed carries out on input lines. -e (a sed command line option) is one way of adding commands to the script. For example, '-e s/A/B/' appends the command 's/A/B/' to the script.

For a very simple sed script, -e is not needed:

```
$ echo old | sed 's/old/new/'
new
$ echo old | sed -e 's/old/new/'
new
```

In command #1, sed knows 's/old/new' is the script, because there is no -e or -f option. In #2, -e appends 's/old/new/' to the previously empty script. The net effect of #1 and #2 is the same.

———

-e can be used more than once. Suppose you want to change 'o' to '=', and 'U' to '-'. It can be done using multiple -e options:

sed s Command (substitute)

```
$ sed -e s/o/=/ -e s/U/-/ rgb
l=wer (#1): "red green blue"
-PPER (#2): "RED GREEN BLUE"
```

- -e appends 's/o/=/' to script.
- -e appends 's/U/-/' to script.

♦ Read line #1 into PatSpace.
♦ Run script. AutoPrint PatSpace.
♦ Read line #2 into PatSpace.
♦ Run script. AutoPrint PatSpace.

; sed Command Line Syntax

Within a sed script, GNU sed and other modern sed versions allow you to usually separate commands with ';' (semicolon). Again, suppose you want to change 'o' to '=', and 'U' to '-'. It can be done as follows:

```
$ sed 's/o/=/; s/U/-/' rgb
l=wer (#1): "red green blue"
-PPER (#2): "RED GREEN BLUE"
```

- Append 's/o/=/' and 's/U/-/' to script.

♦ Read line #1 into PatSpace.
♦ Run script. AutoPrint PatSpace.
♦ Read line #2 into PatSpace.
♦ Run script. AutoPrint PatSpace.

For adding sed commands, ';' is usually shorter and preferred to multiple -e options:

```
sed -e s/X/=/ -e s/A/B/ -e s/1/2/
sed 's/X/=/; s/A/B/; s/1/2/'
```

A few sed commands, such as r, R, w, and W (see Chapter 14) cannot be followed by ';', because the ';' would get confused with the command itself. In that case, separate -e flags would be used.

Chapter 2

If using ';' between commands, putting a space after ';' takes a little more space, but can increase readability:

```
sed 's/X/=/;s/A/B/;s/1/2/'
sed 's/X/=/; s/A/B/; s/1/2/'
```

-f sed Command Line Option

The 'sed script' is the list of commands that sed carries out on input lines. sed allows commands to be placed into separate files, and appended to the current script with the -f option.

Using -f facilitates writing scripts with many lines, and avoids the problems sometimes encountered with quoting command line sed scripts (see Chapter 19). However, -f may require you to keep track of a separate file, which can be a negative.

Suppose s1.sed contains the sed commands shown below:

```
$ cat s1.sed
s/red/333/
s/GREEN/55555/
```

Now, '-f s1.sed' appends the two s commands in s1.sed to the sed script:

```
$ sed -f s1.sed rgb
lower (#1): "333 green blue"
UPPER (#2): "RED 55555 BLUE"
```

To illustrate more how PatSpace is edited, suppose s2.sed contains two sed commands, and is run on 'blue' input text:

sed s Command (substitute)

```
$ cat s2.sed
s/blue/AAAA/
s/AAAA/ZZZZ/
```

```
$ echo blue | sed -f s2.sed
ZZZZ
```

sed commands only see PatSpace, not the input line. At the start of the Cycle, the input 'blue' is read into PatSpace. The first s changes 'blue' to 'AAAA'. Now PatSpace is 'AAAA', so the second s changes 'AAAA' to 'ZZZZ'.

Commands in a separate file should **not** be surrounded by quotes. The following quoted lines in s2.sed would cause an error:

```
's/blue/AAAA/'
's/AAAA/ZZZZ/'
```

sed Output to File or stdout

'stdout' (standard output) is the destination for output printed by sed. In the example below, stdout is sent to the computer screen:

```
$ sed 's/RED/123/' rgb
lower (#1): "red green blue"
UPPER (#2): "123 GREEN BLUE"
```

---

stdout can also be redirected to a file, such as temp in the example below. The mv (move) command then overwrites the original file:

```
$ sed 's/A/B/' in.txt > temp
$ mv temp in.txt
```

Chapter 2

Another possibility is to modify the output in some other way before saving. For example, stdout could be sent through a '|' pipe to the sort command:

```
$ sed s/A/B/ a.txt | sort > x
$ mv x a.txt
```

Note: 'sed s/A/B/ a.txt | sort > a.txt' (trying to do it all on one line) does **not** work correctly. The shell truncates (makes empty) a.txt before sed starts.

sed is "line oriented". sed reads an input line, makes any requested edits, prints the result (unless -n command line option), and then reads the next line.

If you are adding a new paragraph to a book, or writing a new source code function, you will of course use vi, emacs, or other editor.

The utility of sed is typically: 1) repeatedly applying an automatic process, such as converting a file to another format, or 2) editing many files, such as globally changing a variable name. Here is a simplified shell script for editing many files:

```
for file in `cat $list`; do
  sed -f a.sed $file > temp.x
  mv temp.x $file
done
```

Setup and error-checking code has been omitted from the example shell script. At a minimum, if sed exits with an error, abort the shell script, before over-writing the input files:

```
sed -f a.sed $file > temp.x
if [ $?  -ne 0 ]; then
  echo $error_msg; exit 1
fi
```

sed s Command (substitute)

-i sed Command Line Option

The previous section introduced using mv to overwrite the original input file, after sed has done its edits:

```
$ sed 's/A/B/' in.txt > temp
$ mv temp in.txt
```

If you set special file permissions, a drawback of the above method is that the file permissions may be changed. An alternative, to usually retain the file permissions, is as follows:

```
$ cp in.txt temp
$ sed 's/A/B/' temp > in.txt
```

The -i (--in-place) command line option is a better way to ensure the file permissions do not change. -i tells sed to edit the file 'in place'.

Behind the scenes, sed makes a temporary file to store the intermediate results. As shown below, -i results in much shorter and easier-to-read code:

```
$ sed -i 's/A/B/' in.txt
```

A potential drawback of -i is that there are no user-specified intermediate files for you to examine if needed.

Of course, -i only works when input is from a file. If input is from stdin, using -i will produce an error.

Conveniently, -i can be used to edit several text files 'in place', using one sed command:

```
$ sed -i s/A/B/ 1.txt 2.txt 3.txt
```

Without the -i option, the input files would be 'glommed' together, edited as one stream. With the -i option, each input file is retained and edited 'in place', using a single sed command.

Chapter 2

Regardless of how you overwrite the input file (mv, cp, -i), it is usually a good idea to have some kind of backup to revert to in case you make a mistake and damage the input file.

sed (and other Unix utilities) are very powerful and sharp tools. Used with care, they save huge amounts of time and energy. Used irresponsibly, they can cause huge amounts of damage.

It is wise to keep the following in mind and take preventive steps: 'There are two kinds of computer users: Those who have lost data, and those who are going to lose data'.

3: Flags for s (substitute) Command

This chapter explains 'flags' for the s (substitute) command:

```
i   Ignore case when matching
g   Global substitution on line
n   Number of match to change
p   Print the result if match
w   Write result to file if match
e   Execute PatSpace to PatSpace
m   Multi-Line Mode Matching
```

Here is an example s command, without flags:

```
$ echo old old | sed s/old/new/
new old
```

The result is 'new old' (not 'new new'). Unless we tell it otherwise, the s command changes only the **first** match it finds on a line.

To allow multiple substitutions, and other added capabilities, the s command takes 'flags', as listed above and explained in this chapter.

A more complete syntax for the s command, including the flags, can be written as:

```
s/RegEx/SubEx/[flags]
```

's/RegEx/SubEx/[flags]' searches for RegEx in PatSpace, and replaces ('substitutes') one or more matching portions of PatSpace with SubEx. The s command 'finds and replaces'.

The [flags] are optional. Each flag, if included, turns on a particular setting.

Chapter 3

i (ignore case) Flag

The i (ignore case) flag for the s command tells sed to ignore uppercase vs lowercase when looking for a match in PatSpace. The flag can be 'i' or 'I' (capital eye). 'i' is preferred.

```
$ echo old | sed s/Old/xxx/
old
```

Because 'i' flag is **not** used:

- RegEx 'Old' does **not** match 'old'.
- So s does not replace 'old'.

```
$ echo old | sed s/Old/xxx/i
xxx
```

Because 'i' flag **is** used:

- RegEx 'Old' matches 'old'.
- So s changes 'old' to 'xxx'.

You can also ignore case by using a RegEx such as [aA][bB] (explained in Chapter 4). But the i flag is simpler and easier to read:

```
$ echo ab | sed s/AB/=/i
=
$ echo ab | sed s/[aA][bB]/=/
=
```

Flags for s (substitute) Command

g (global) and n (number) Flags

```
g   Changes all matches
n   Changes match #n
```

The g (global) flag for the s command tells sed to change **all** matches, not just the first match.

```
$ echo old old | sed s/old/new/g
new new
```

The RegEx 'old' matches twice in 'old old' PatSpace. The g flag tells s to substitute 'new' for 'old' both times.

```
$ echo aaaaa | sed s/a/+/
+aaaa
$ echo aaaaa | sed s/a/+/g
+++++
```

The example above contrasts:

- g flag omitted (replace match #1)
- g flag used (replace all 5 matches)

The n (number) flag for the s command tells sed to change one specified match, instead of match #1. A number, such as 2 or 3, is substituted for n.

```
$ echo old old | sed s/old/new/2
old new
```

- n flag (value = 2) is used.
- So 'old' #2 is changed to 'new'.

Chapter 3

```
$ echo aaaaa | sed s/a/=/
=aaaa
$ echo aaaaa | sed s/a/=/3
aa=aa
```

The example above contrasts:

- n flag omitted (replace match #1)
- n (3) flag used (replace match #3)

If n is 'too large', no replacement occurs:

```
$ echo aaaaa | sed s/a/=/9
aaaaa
```

The default action (no g or n flags) is to change the first match. So the commands 's/a/=/1' and 's/a/=/' have the same effect.

n can be large, if needed. So 's/old/new/1000' is a valid (but unlikely) s command.

-n sed Command Line Option

Normally, sed 'AutoPrints' PatSpace at the end of the sed script, before reading the next input line. sed -n turns off AutoPrint. So the following (useless) command produces no output:

```
$ echo old | sed -n s/old/new/
```

If you use the -n option, to do anything useful, you **must** also use some other way to produce output, such as the p flag (next section).

-n used in isolation does not make sense. In contrast, -n used in combination with the p flag (and a few other sed commands), lets you fine tune when sed produces output.

Flags for s (substitute) Command

p (print) and w (write) Flags

```
p  Print the result if match
w  Write result to file if match
```

The p (print) flag for the s command prints PatSpace to stdout, after replacement, **if** a replacement was done.

The p flag is usually used along with the -n command line option (previous section). So it makes sense to discuss the p flag and -n option together.

Here are some examples that show how '-n option' and 'p flag' work together:

```
$ sed 's/RED/xxx/' rgb
lower (#1): "red green blue"
UPPER (#2): "xxx GREEN BLUE"
```

- s command only changed line #2.
- sed AutoPrints both lines.

```
$ sed -n 's/RED/xxx/p' rgb
UPPER (#2): "xxx GREEN BLUE"
```

- s command only changed line #2.
- PatSpace does not AutoPrint (-n flag).
- p flag caused line #2 to print.

23

Chapter 3

Keep in mind that the -n option and the p flag do not 'know about' each other. The two are often used in combination, but operate separately.

This is shown by the following example, which prints 'xxx' twice ('p flag' and AutoPrint):

```
$ echo ABC | sed s/ABC/xxx/p
xxx
xxx
```

- 'ABC' is read into PatSpace.
- PatSpace is changed to 'xxx'.
- PatSpace is printed (p flag).
- AutoPrint PatSpace (no -n).

The w (write) flag for the s command writes PatSpace to a file, after replacement, **if** a replacement was done.

```
$ sed -n 's/red/xxx/w a.txt' rgb
$ cat a.txt
lower (#1): "xxx green blue"
```

- s command only changed line #1.
- No lines AutoPrint (-n).
- w flag wrote line #1 PatSpace to 'a.txt'.

If a.txt previously exists, it is truncated at sed startup. Each time w runs, it appends PatSpace (after replacement) to the a.txt file.

Put one space between the w flag and the file name. It is better style, and some versions of sed may get confused if you use two spaces.

A minor point: Do not put spaces (or the ';' command separator) after the file name. The w flag is very literal, and will incorporate a trailing space or ';' into the file name.

Flags for s (substitute) Command

e (execute) and m (multi) Flags

```
e  Execute PatSpace to PatSpace
m  Multi-Line mode matching
```

The 'e' and 'm' s command flags are used less often than the previous flags. Both flags are GNU extensions. If you are relatively new to sed, you might skip the e and m flags for now (go the next section).

The e (execute) flag for the s command executes PatSpace as a command, **if** a substitution was made. The command output is copied back into PatSpace.

In the next example, the Unix 'expr' command can be placed into PatSpace ('&' in the SubEx is explained in Chapter 9). Then, the e flag runs 'expr' to do math (add 2 and 4):

```
$ echo 2 | sed 's/./expr & + 4/e'
6
```

- '2' is read into PatSpace.
- s replaces '2' with 'expr 2 + 4'.
- e flag runs PatSpace as command.
- '6' is saved to PatSpace. sed AutoPrints.

Chapter 3

Here are more examples of placing the expr command into PatSpace, and using the e flag to run PatSpace. If these are not clear, come back later or skip this section, because the e flag is rarely used.

```
$ seq 3 | sed 's/./expr & \\* 5/e'
5
10
15
```

```
$ seq 3 | sed 's/./expr & \\* &/e'
1
4
9
```

The m (multi-line) flag for the s command triggers 'multi-line mode':
^ also matches the empty string after a newline, and $ also matches the empty string before a newline.

At this point, we have not discussed multi-line operations. So you may want to come back to this section later, or skip it, because the m flag is not used very much. Chapter 5 explains about ^ and $ characters (start and end of PatSpace).

In each example below, N appends the second line of input to create '1\n2' PatSpace:

```
$ seq 2 | sed 'N; s/^2/=/m'
1
=
```

The example above, using the m flag, triggers multi-line mode, so '^2' matches '2' in '1\n2'.

```
$ seq 2 | sed 'N; s/^2/=/'
1
2
```

Flags for s (substitute) Command

This second example does not use the m flag. So multi-line mode is not used, and '^2' does not match within '1\n2'.

Combining s Command Flags

Any flag for the s command may be combined with any other flag, with a few special cases:

1) The w flag **must** come last, followed by a file name. For example, 'w' comes after 'g' in 's/old/new/gw a.txt'.

2) Do **not** use the same flag more than once. For example, 's/A/B/gg' produces an error message.

3) Combining n and g tells sed to change match occurrences n, n+1, n+2, etc.

Below are examples of combining flags:

```
$ sed 's/r/+/ig' rgb
lowe+ (#1): "+ed g+een blue"
UPPE+ (#2): "+ED G+EEN BLUE"
```

- Match either 'r' or 'R' (i flag).
- Change all matches (g flag).

```
$ sed -n 's/e/+/gp' rgb
low+r (#1): "r+d gr++n blu+"
```

- Change all 'e' to '+' (g flag).
- PatSpace does not AutoPrint (-n option).
- Print PatSpace if changed by s (p flag).

Chapter 3

```
$ sed -n 's/E/+/2p' rgb
UPPER (#2): "R+D GREEN BLUE"
```

- Only change match #2 (n flag).
- PatSpace does not AutoPrint (-n option).
- Print PatSpace if changed by s (p flag).

```
$ sed -n 's/e/+/gw a.txt' rgb
$ cat a.txt
low+r (#1): "r+d gr++n blu+"
```

- Change all 'e' to '+' (g flag).
- PatSpace does not AutoPrint (-n flag).
- Write PatSpace if changed by s (w flag).

```
$ sed 's/[aeiou]/+/3g' rgb
lower (#1): "r+d gr++n bl++"
UPPER (#2): "RED GREEN BLUE"
```

- Change vowel #3 to '+' (n flag).
- Change vowel #4, #5, etc. (g flag).

To review, 's/RegEx/SubEx/[flags]' is the basic syntax for the s (substitute) command. This chapter explained and illustrated the optional flags for the s command.

Now that you have learned the s command, we can explain about 'MetaChars' (next chapters), to add flexibility and power to regular expressions.

4: Single Character MetaChars

```
      Z          The Letter Z
      .          Any Character
     \.          Literal Period
     \w          Word Character
     \W          Non-Word Char
 [[:upper:]]     One of A-Z
    [A-Z]        One of A-Z
    [^A-Z]       not A-Z
```

This chapter covers 'Literal' characters and single character 'MetaChars' (metacharacters) in a RegEx (regular expression).

As shown in the list above, a character in a RegEx can range in complexity from the simple Literal 'Z', to the complex MetaChar '[^A-Z]'.

A Literal like 'Z' is easy to understand. A MetaChar like '[^A-Z]' is harder to understand. We offer many MetaChar examples to help learn.

Mastering the powerful s (substitute) command (Chapters 1-3) is the most important step to learning sed. Using flexible MetaChars within a RegEx (Chapters 4-9) is the second most important step.

Literal Character in RegEx

Even the simple Literal 'am' is a RegEx, though an inflexible one. 'am' matches 'am', and nothing else.

Suppose PatSpace contains 'Madam', and we want to replace 'am' (the RegEx) with 'cap' (the SubEx). Here is how sed does it, step by step:

```
$ echo Madam | sed 's/am/cap/'
Madcap
```

Chapter 4

```
Madam
am
```

- Read 'Madam' into PatSpace.
- Align 'am' with PatSpace letter #1 (M).
- 'a' matches 'M'? No. Give up on match.

```
Madam
 am
```

- Align 'am' with PatSpace letter #2 (a).
- 'a' matches 'a'? Yes. A match so far!
- 'm' matches 'd'? No. Give up on match.

```
Madam
  am
```

- Align 'am' with PatSpace letter #3 (d).
- 'a' matches 'd'? No. Give up on match.

```
Madam
   am
```

- Align 'am' with PatSpace letter #4 (a).
- 'a' matches 'a'? Yes. A match so far!
- 'm' matches 'm'? Yes. It is a match!
- s command replaces 'am' with 'cap'.

Single Character MetaChars

Does 'am' match 'Madam'? Only partially. 'am' really only matches 'am' in 'Madam'. So s only replaces 'am' (the matching portion). The result is 'Madcap'.

Keep in mind: 1) sed looks for a match in the current PatSpace, **not** the original line. 2) The match may be limited to a portion of PatSpace. 3) If the g flag is used, there may be several matches replaced.

You can do a lot with a RegEx that is totally Literal. For example, sed lets you change 'b1_MakeList' to 'b1_Display', in many files, in many directories.

However, 'b1_MakeListing' may also exist. This could get changed to 'b1_Displaying' by mistake. Later, we explain ways to use 'MetaChars' within a RegEx, so you get exactly the changes you want.

GNU sed also includes some special Literal characters, as listed below:

```
\a   Alert (ASCII 7)
\n   Newline (ASCII 10)
\f   Form Feed (ASCII 12)
\r   Carriage Return (ASCII 13)
\t   Horizontal Tab (ASCII 9)
\v   Vertical Tab (ASCII 11)
```

```
\d010   Decimal 010 (ASCII 10)
\o012   Octal 012 (ASCII 10)
\x0A    Hex 0A (ASCII 10)
```

For completeness, there are also special '\c' control characters. '\ca' and '\cA' both translate to Ctrl-A (ASCII 1). '\cz' and '\cZ' both translate to Ctrl-Z (ASCII 26).

Other more obscure control characters are allowed, such as '\c;' (ASCII 123). For more information, refer to the GNU sed manual.

Literals like '\c;' are not recommended, because they are confusing. Use an equivalent clearer form, such as '\d123' or '\x7B'.

Chapter 4

. (Wildcard Character)

A MetaChar (metacharacter) is a special symbol that represents something else. MetaChars create flexible and powerful regular expressions.

'.' (dot) is the simplest MetaChar, and is used often. Use '.' to match **any** single character, even a newline.

Using '.' (instead of a Literal) expands the number of potential matches. A RegEx including '.' can match **many** patterns, perhaps more than intended.

For example, 'hat' matches a few (underlined) PatSpace segments: hat, hatch, shatter, etc.

In contrast, 'h.t' matches many more segments: hat, hit, hot, hatch, hutch, shatter, shutter, etc.

In addition, 'h.t' matches segments of nonsense sequences: h5t, h=t, hjt, h5tch, h=tch, sh=tter, etc.

Here are 2 examples using '.' in sed:

Replace 'l.' (ell followed by a character) with '++':

```
$ sed 's/l./++/g' rgb
++wer (#1): "red green b++e"
UPPER (#2): "RED GREEN BLUE"
```

Replace '.E' (character followed by E) with '++':

```
$ sed 's/.E/++/g' rgb
lower (#1): "red green blue"
UP++R (#2): "++D G++EN BL++"
```

Note: After 'RE' in GREEN is replaced with '++', the next candidate to replace is 'EN' (not '+E'). 'EN' does not match '.E'.

\ (Specify Literal Character)

Suppose you wanted to look for an actual period, such as a decimal point. Because '.' is a MetaChar, the following attempt works poorly:

Single Character MetaChars

```
$ echo 1.3 | sed 's/1.3/1.4/'
1.4
$ echo 103 | sed 's/1.3/1.4/'
1.4
```

- '103' also matches the RegEx '1.3'
- So '103' is mistakenly changed to '1.4'

To solve this problem, '\.' represents a Literal period. '\' is the BackSlash (or escape) character. Thus, the above example would properly be written as:

```
$ echo 1.3 | sed 's/1\.3/1.4/'
1.4
$ echo 103 | sed 's/1\.3/1.4/'
103
```

This time, 103 does not match, so is not replaced.

Here are additional MetaChars (described later) that may be treated as Literals by placing '\' in front of the MetaChar:

```
MetaChar:    *    ^    $    [
Literal:    \*   \^   \$   \[
```

'\' is used in a Windows directory path. To place '\' itself in the RegEx, precede '\' with another backslash, as in the following example:

```
$ echo 'd:\a' | sed 's_d:\\_e:\\_'
e:\a
```

This changes 'd:\' to 'e:\'. Note that '_' instead of '/' was used as the Delimiter, to make the command easier to read (but still unavoidably somewhat obscure).

Chapter 4

[ ] (Character Set)

So far, we have learned two extremes: The Literal 'x' only matches 'x'. The wildcard '.' matches any character.

A 'character set' gives you an intermediate capability, to specify more than one character, but fewer than all characters.

A character set matches any character in a bracket-enclosed list. For example, [aeiou] matches any vowel:

```
$ echo abet | sed s/[aeiou]/=/g
=b=t
```

```
$ sed s/[aeiou]/+/g rgb
l+w+r (#1): "r+d gr++n bl++"
UPPER (#2): "RED GREEN BLUE"
```

Any character matching [aeiou] (any vowel) is changed to '+'.

[0123456789] matches any single digit. This can be written more concisely as [0-9], which matches 0, 9, and 'everything in between':

```
$ echo K1847 | sed 's/[0-9]/x/g'
Kxxxx
$ echo K1847 | sed 's/[0-4]/x/g'
Kx8x7
```

```
$ sed 's/[0-9]/X/' rgb
lower (#X): "red green blue"
UPPER (#X): "RED GREEN BLUE"
```

[a-z] means a lowercase letter (a, z, and 'everything in between'). [A-Z] means an uppercase letter.

Single Character MetaChars

```
$ sed 's/[a-z]/-/g' rgb
----- (#1): "--- ----- ----"
UPPER (#2): "RED GREEN BLUE"
```

```
$ sed 's/[A-Z]/-/g' rgb
lower (#1): "red green blue"
----- (#2): "--- ----- ----"
```

```
$ sed 's/[A-M]/-/g' rgb
lower (#1): "red green blue"
UPP-R (#2): "R-- -R--N --U-"
```

Sequences like a-z and 0-9 may be combined into more complex sets. For example:

```
[a-zA-Z]        alphabetic
[a-zA-Z_]       alphabetic or _
[a-zA-Z0-9]     alphanumeric
[a-zA-Z0-9_]    alphanumeric or _
```

If '^' follows the opening bracket, the sense of the match is reversed. With a leading '^', the match is for any character **not** in the set:

```
[^aeiou]    not a vowel
[^0-9]      not a 0-9 digit
```

To include ']' in the character set, place it as far to the left as possible:

```
[])}]       ], ), or }
[^])}]      not ], ), or }
```

Chapter 4

To include '-' in the character set, place it as far to the left or right as possible:

```
[0-9]     digit
[-0-9]    digit or '-'
[0-9-]    digit or '-'
```

Among other uses, [^] can define the end of a matching segment, as in the following contrasting examples:

```
$ sed 's/e.*e/++++/' rgb
low++++"
UPPER (#2): "RED GREEN BLUE"
```

```
$ sed 's/e[^e]*e/++++/' rgb
low++++d green blue"
UPPER (#2): "RED GREEN BLUE"
```

'e.*e' means: 'e', then 0 or more any character, then 'e' again. The more specific 'e[^e]*e' means: 'e', then 0 or more **not** 'e', then 'e' again.

If this does not make sense right now, come back to it later after Chapter 6 explains the '*' MetaChar. It is really important you eventually understand the second example, because the idea is so useful.

\w \W (Word and Non-Word)

'\w' and '\W' are conveniences, synonyms for certain character classes.

'\w' matches any 'Word' character.
'\w' and '[a-zA-Z0-9_]' are the same.

'\W' matches any 'non-Word' character.
'\W' and '[^a-zA-Z0-9_]' are the same.

Single Character MetaChars

A sed 'Word' is a sequence of [a-zA-Z0-9_] characters (lowercase, uppercase, digits, '_'). Here are some examples to make it clear:

```
Is one Word     Not one Word
  cat_dog         cat dog
  ab_Ab_12        ab.AB.12
  bit_flag        bit-flag
```

- Note: '-' is **not** a Word character.
- 'A-B-C' counts as Word-Word-Word.
- 'A_B_C' is counted as one Word.

```
$ sed 's!\w\w\w\w\w!=!'  rgb
= (#1): "red green blue"
= (#2): "RED GREEN BLUE"
```

- Each line is read into PatSpace.
- 'lower' matches '\w\w\w\w\w'.
- 'UPPER' matches '\w\w\w\w\w'.
- Each match is changed to '='.
- AutoPrint PatSpace both times.

```
$ sed 's!r\w!++!'  rgb
lower (#1): "++d green blue"
UPPER (#2): "RED GREEN BLUE"
```

- Line #1 is read into PatSpace.
- 'r ' (r space) does not match 'r\w'.
- 're' matches 'r\w', is changed to '++'.
- AutoPrint PatSpace.

♦ Line #2 is read into PatSpace.
♦ 'r\w' not found. AutoPrint PatSpace.

Chapter 4

```
$ sed 's!u\w\W!\U&!'  rgb
lower (#1): "red green blUE"
UPPER (#2): "RED GREEN BLUE"
```

- Line #1 is read into PatSpace.
- 'ue"' matches 'u\w\W,' is made upper.
- AutoPrint PatSpace.
- Line #2 does not match 'u\w\W'.

[: :] (Posix Character Class)

   Posix character classes ensure that matches are done consistently in different locales. For example, Ñ (N with tilde) is included in [:alpha:] in the Spanish locale.
   A Posix character class has a special syntax. [:lower:] by itself does not work, at least not as expected. The Posix character class must be within square brackets, such as [[:lower:]].

   Explanations in this section use the familiar sample input shown below, and show the equivalent character sets for US English users.

```
$ cat rgb
lower (#1): "red green blue"
UPPER (#2): "RED GREEN BLUE"
```

[:alnum:] matches a letter or number.
[[:alnum:]] is the same as [a-zA-Z0-9].

```
$ sed s/[[:alnum:]]/-/g rgb
----- (#-): "--- ----- ----"
----- (#-): "--- ----- ----"
```

[:alpha:] matches an alphabetic character.
[[:alpha:]] is the same as [a-zA-Z].

Single Character MetaChars

```
$ sed s/[[:alpha:]]/-/g rgb
----- (#1): "--- ----- ----"
----- (#2): "--- ----- ----"
```

[:blank:] matches a space or tab.
[[:blank:]] is the same as [\t].

```
$ sed s/[[:blank:]]/-/g rgb
lower-(#1):-"red-green-blue"
UPPER-(#2):-"RED-GREEN-BLUE"
```

[:cntrl:] matches a control character.
[[:cntrl:]] is the same as [\x00-\x1F\x7F].

```
$ sed s/[[:cntrl:]]/-/g rgb
lower (#1): "red green blue"
UPPER (#2): "RED GREEN BLUE"
```

[:digit:] matches a numerical digit.
[[:digit:]] is the same as [0-9].

```
$ sed s/[[:digit:]]/-/g rgb
lower (#-): "red green blue"
UPPER (#-): "RED GREEN BLUE"
```

[:graph:] matches a visible character.
[[:graph:]] is the same as [\x21-\x7E].

```
$ sed s/[[:graph:]]/-/g rgb
----- ----- ---- ----- -----
----- ----- ---- ----- -----
```

Chapter 4

[:lower:] matches a lower case letter.
[[:lower:]] is the same as [a-z].

```
$ sed s/[[:lower:]]/-/g rgb
----- (#1): "--- ----- ----"
UPPER (#2): "RED GREEN BLUE"
```

[:print:] matches a visible character, or 'space'.
[[:print:]] is the same as [\x20-\x7E].

```
$ sed s/[[:print:]]/-/g rgb
---------------------------
---------------------------
```

[:punct:] matches punctuation or a symbol:

```
 !  "  #  $  %  &  '  (  )  *
 +  ,  -  .  /  :  ;  <  =  >  ?
 @  [  \  ]  ^  _  `  {  |  }  ~
```

```
$ sed s/[[:punct:]]/-/g rgb
lower --1-- -red green blue-
UPPER --2-- -RED GREEN BLUE-
```

[:space:] matches a whitespace character.
[[:space:]] is the same as [\t\r\n\v\f].

```
$ sed s/[[:space:]]/-/g rgb
lower-(#1):-"red-green-blue"
UPPER-(#2):-"RED-GREEN-BLUE"
```

Single Character MetaChars

[:upper:] matches an upper case letter.
[[:upper:]] is the same as [A-Z].

```
$ sed s/[[:upper:]]/-/g rgb
lower (#1): "red green blue"
----- (#2): "--- ----- ----"
```

[:xdigit:] matches a hexadecimal digit.
[[:xdigit:]] is the same as [A-Fa-f0-9].

```
$ sed s/[[:xdigit:]]/-/g rgb
low-r (#-): "r-- gr--n -lu-"
UPP-R (#-): "R-- GR--N -LU-"
```

Posix character classes may be combined with other characters, or other classes. For example:

```
Character class     Equivalent
[[:digit:]ab]       [0-9ab]
[[:lower:]12]       [a-z12]
```

5: Anchor MetaChars

This chapter discusses 'Anchor MetaChars'. An Anchor MetaChar does not occupy space, and does not match a character. Instead, it matches a boundary:

```
^     Start of PatSpace
$     End of PatSpace

\<    Start of Word
\>    End of Word

\b    Is Word Boundary
\B    Is not Word Boundary
```

^ (Start of PatSpace)

When used at the start of a RegEx, ^ does not occupy space, and does not represent a character. Instead, it means 'start of PatSpace'.

```
        What RegEx Matches
^       Start of PatSpace
^X      X at Start of PatSpace
^^      ^ at Start of PatSpace
X^      Literal X^ in PatSpace
```

If the RegEx is solely '^', it matches the start of PatSpace, whatever the contents of PatSpace:

```
$ echo XYZ | sed 's/^/=/'
=XYZ
```

Anchor MetaChars

- XYZ is read into PatSpace.
- ^ matches 'start of PatSpace'.
- s inserts '=' at start of PatSpace.

If ^ starts the RegEx, followed by a character 'X', ^ anchors 'X' to the start of PatSpace:

```
$ echo XYZ | sed 's/^X/=/'
=YZ
```

- 'X' is at start of PatSpace.
- So '^X' matches X in 'XYZ'.
- s replaces anchored 'X' with '='.

```
$ echo XYZ | sed 's/^Y/=/'
XYZ
```

- 'Y' is **not** at start of PatSpace.
- So '^Y' does not match Y in 'XYZ'.
- So s does not do replacement.

If ^ is **not** the first character in the RegEx, ^ is interpreted as a Literal:

```
$ echo 2^3=8 | sed 's/2^3/8/'
8=8
```

- Literal '2^3=8' is read into PatSpace.
- ^ is **not** first character in RegEx.
- So ^ in '2^3' RegEx is 'Literal ^'.
- So s replaces '2^3' with '8'.

Chapter 5

Sometimes, you may need to match for a Literal ˆ at the start of PatSpace. The first attempt fails, the second attempt works:

```
$ echo ˆHDR | sed 's/ˆHDR/=/'
ˆHDR
```

- Literal 'ˆHDR' is read into PatSpace.
- ˆ in RegEx means 'start of PatSpace'.
- But 'HDR' is **not** start of PatSpace.
- So s does not do replacement.

```
$ echo ˆHDR | sed 's/ˆˆHDR/=/'
=
```

- Again, 'ˆHDR' is read into PatSpace.
- 'ˆˆ' means 'ˆ at Start of PatSpace'.
- PatSpace is 'ˆHDR', matches RegEx.
- So s replaces 'ˆHDR' with '='.

$ (End of PatSpace)

When used at the end of a RegEx, $ does not occupy space, and does not represent a character. Instead, it means 'end of PatSpace'.

```
        What RegEx Matches
$       End of PatSpace
Z$      Z at End of PatSpace
$$      $ at End of PatSpace
$Z      Literal $Z in PatSpace
```

You can think of ˆ and $ as matching bookends, marking the start and end of PatSpace.

If the RegEx is solely $, it matches the end of PatSpace, whatever the contents of PatSpace:

Anchor MetaChars

```
$ echo XYZ | sed 's/$/=/'
XYZ=
```

- 'XYZ' is read into PatSpace.
- $ means 'end of PatSpace'.
- s inserts '=' at end of PatSpace.

If $ ends the RegEx, preceded by a character 'Z', $ anchors 'Z' to the end of PatSpace:

```
$ echo XYZ | sed 's/Z$/=/'
XY=
```

- 'Z' is at end of PatSpace.
- So 'Z$' matches Z in 'XYZ'.
- s replaces anchored 'Z' with '='.

```
$ echo XYZ | sed 's/Y$/=/'
XYZ
```

- 'Y' is **not** at end of PatSpace.
- So 'Y$' does not match Y in 'XYZ'.
- So s does not do replacement.

If $ is not the last character in the RegEx, $ is interpreted as the Literal $ character:

```
$ echo '$2=99' | sed 's/$2/$4/'
$4=99
```

- '$2=99' is read into PatSpace.
- '$2' RegEx means 'Literal $2'.
- s replaces '$2' in PatSpace with '$4'.

45

Chapter 5

Note: The $ examples above require 'single quotes' to work correctly. This is one reason to normally use single quotes.

$2 (unquoted) and "$2" are both interpreted by the Unix shell as a shell variable. '$2' is protected from interpretation by the shell, and **not** treated as a shell variable.

Together, ^ and $ can find blank lines. In the example below, s changes the blank line to '=':

```
$ echo -e "\nA"

A
```

```
$ echo -e "\nA" | sed 's/^$/=/'
=
A
```

\< \> \b (Word Boundaries)

Suppose you want to match 'cow' and change to 'ox'. Here is a simple attempt:

```
$ echo cow | sed s/cow/ox/
ox
$ echo scow | sed s/cow/ox/
sox
```

It does not work well. It finds 'cow' within 'scow' (or 'cowl', etc.), resulting in nonsense changes.

Using ' cow ' (spaces around cow) instead of 'cow' corrects the case with 'scow', but fails in other cases, such as the following lines:

```
Please yoke the cow.
'cow' is a noun.
An 'oxcen' (female cow).
```

A similar problem occurs with variable and function names, because of overlaps between names.

For example, we want to change 'mps' to 'mph', but **not** change 'amps' to 'amph'. Or we want to change 'maxVal' to 'MaxVal', but **not** change 'climaxVal' to 'cliMaxVal'.

Fortunately, sed allows you to match 'Word' boundaries, using '\<' and '\>' metacharacters.

```
\<    Word starts
\>    Word ends
```

The correct way to carry out our 'cow' to 'ox' substitution is:

```
$ echo cow | sed 's/\<cow\>/ox/'
ox
$ echo scow | sed 's/\<cow\>/ox/'
scow
```

'\<' and '\>' mark the boundaries of 'Words'. What is a 'Word', according to sed?

As previously explained, a Word is a sequence of [a-zA-Z0-9_] characters (lowercase, uppercase, digits, and '_'). Again, here are some examples to make it clear:

```
Is one Word      Not one Word
  cat_dog          cat dog
  ab_Ab_12         ab.AB.12
  bit_flag         bit-flag
```

- Note that '-' is not a Word character.
- 'A-B-C' counts as Word-Word-Word.
- 'A_B_C' is counted as one Word.

'at' is a Word. But 'at' within 'cat' is **not** a Word. The sequence of Word characters extends as far as possible to define the Word.

Chapter 5

'\b' is similar to '\<' and '\>', described above. '\b' indicates **either** start (\<) or end (\>) of a Word, depending on whether a Word character comes before or after.

```
$ echo cow | sed 's/\bcow/ox/'
ox
$ echo scow | sed 's/\bcow/ox/'
scow
```

```
$ sed 's/r\b/=/i' rgb
lowe= (#1): "red green blue"
UPPE= (#2): "RED GREEN BLUE"
```

```
$ sed 's/\br/=/i' rgb
lower (#1): "=ed green blue"
UPPER (#2): "=ED GREEN BLUE"
```

```
$ sed 's/\b/=/7g' rgb
lower (#1): "red =green= =blue="
UPPER (#2): "RED =GREEN= =BLUE="
```

Whether to use '\<Word\>' or '\bWord\b' is your personal preference.

———

Note: '\<' and '\>' (as well as '\b') always include the BackSlash ('\'), even if you use the -r flag (Chapter 6).

\B (Not a Word Boundary)

'\B' is the opposite of '\b'. '\B' matches only if **not** a Word boundary.

```
$ echo cow | sed 's/\Bcow/++/'
cow
$ echo scow | sed 's/\Bcow/++/'
s++
```

- '\Bcow' does not match PatSpace 'cow'.
- '\Bcow' matches 'cow' in 'scow'.

```
$ echo cow | sed 's/cow\B/++/'
cow
$ echo cowl | sed 's/cow\B/++/'
++l
```

- 'cow\B' does not match PatSpace 'cow'.
- 'cow\B' matches 'cow' in 'cowl'.

6: Simple Repetition MetaChars

Repetition MetaChars specify how many times the preceding character, character set, or grouping is repeated. There are two categories of repetition MetaChars:

```
Simple:   *  \+  \?

General:  \{N\} \{L,\} \{L,H\}
```

This chapter explains the simple ones; the next chapter covers the general ones. Here are the simple repetition MetaChars:

```
*    0 or more of previous
\+   1 or more of previous
\?   0 or 1 of previous
```

* (0 or More of Previous)

* is the most commonly used repetition MetaChar. * means 0 or more of the preceding character, character set, or group. For example, 'x*' means '0 or more x'.

'.*' (dot star) means '0 or more of any character'. So it always matches the entire PatSpace (unless PatSpace includes malformed multi-byte characters):

```
$ echo aB3!^_=+ | sed s/.*/=/
=
$ echo '' | sed s/.*/=/
=
```

50

Simple Repetition MetaChars

'b*' means '0 or more of b'. 'b*' matches 'nothing', b, bb, etc. So, in both cases below, s replaces 'b*' with '=':

```
$ echo '' | sed 's/b*/=/'
=
$ echo b | sed 's/b*/=/'
=
```

Because 'b*' can match 'nothing', 'b*' always matches the start of PatSpace, even if no b at the start.

In both examples below, s changes 'b*' (zero b at start of PatSpace) to '=':

```
$ echo ab | sed 's/b*/=/'
=ab
$ echo abb | sed 's/b*/=/'
=abb
```

In both examples below (adds g flag), s changes 'b*' (0 or more b) to '=' three times:

```
$ echo abc | sed 's/b*/=/g'
=a=c=
$ echo abbc | sed 's/b*/=/g'
=a=c=
```

- Start of PatSpace matches 'b*' RegEx.
- So s changes 'b*' to '='.
- 'a' does not match 'b*'. No replacement.

♦ b and bb both match 'b*' RegEx.
♦ So s changes 'b*' to '='.

- 'c' does not match 'b*'. No replacement.
- End of PatSpace matches 'b*'.
- So s changes 'b*' to '='.

51

Chapter 6

'bb*' means 'b, then zero or more b'. In contrast with 'b*', 'bb*' does **not** always match the start of PatSpace.

'bb*' matches any time there is at least one 'b' character. So, in each case below, s changes 'bb*' to '=':

```
$ echo ab | sed 's/bb*/=/'
a=
$ echo abbb | sed 's/bb*/=/'
a=
```

In example #2, how does sed know to match (and change) bbb, instead of b or bb? It turns out that * is 'greedy'. All repetition MetaChars are greedy.

'Greedy' means 'matches the maximum number of characters possible'. The match expands to the greatest extent possible.

Because * is greedy, in each case below, 'b*' expands as much as possible.

```
$ echo bc | sed 's/b*/=/'
=c
$ echo bbbc | sed 's/b*/=/'
=c
```

If you are not careful, '.*' can match more than you might expect (such as 'b:c:d:e:f:g' in the following case):

```
$ x=a:b:c:d:e:f:g:h
$ echo $x | sed s/:.*:/:=:/
a:=:h
```

As explained previously (this important concept is worth repeating), you can limit the match extent as follows:

```
$ x=a:b:c:d:e:f:g:h
$ echo $x | sed s/:[^:]*:/:=:/
a:=:c:d:e:f:g:h
```

Using '[^:]*' instead of '.*' limits the match to characters that are **not** ':' (**not** colon).

Here is a final example of how to safely limit the match extent, in case there are several quoted segments in PatSpace:

```
$ sed 's/"[^"]*"/"="/' rgb
lower (#1): "="
UPPER (#2): "="
```

\+ (1 or More of Previous)

The '\+' MetaChar means 1 or more of the preceding character, character set, or group. For example, 'x\+' means '1 or more x'.

This will become clear with some examples. In the following examples, 'b\+' matches b or bbb.

```
$ echo abc | sed 's/b\+/=/'
a=c
$ echo abbbc | sed 's/b\+/=/'
a=c
```

-r sed Command Line Option

It can be an irritation that '\+' (previous section) requires the '\' BackSlash, making the syntax somewhat cluttered and hard to read.

The -r (--regexp-extended) sed command line option lets you write cleaner syntax. With the -r option, '+' now means 'one or more of preceding', and '\+' means the Literal 'plus' character.

Chapter 6

The following examples illustrate -r and '\+'. The first example uses '\+' as the MetaChar; the second example uses '+' as the MetaChar:

```
$ echo abbc | sed 's/b\+/=/'
a=c
$ echo abbc | sed -r 's/b+/=/'
a=c
```

Here are two more examples showing the -r option. The first example uses '+' as the Literal; the second uses '\+' as the Literal:

```
$ echo abb+ | sed 's/b+/=/'
ab=
$ echo abb+ | sed -r 's/b\+/=/'
ab=
```

It is usually better to avoid using the '\' BackSlash, as it makes a RegEx harder to read. 'b+' is easier to read than 'b\+'.

Besides \+, -r lets you remove the BackSlash from \?, \{, \}, \(, \), and \| MetaChars, all explained in later sections. Note that \<, \>, \b and \B Word boundary MetaChars (Chapter 5) always use BackSlash, even if -r is used.

\? (0 or 1 of Previous)

The '\?' MetaChar means 0 or 1 of the preceding character, character set, or group. For example, 'x\?' means 'nothing' or 'x'.

'\?' lets you make a change, whether or not a particular character or group occurs in the RegEx.

Simple Repetition MetaChars

In each example below, PatSpace must contain HA for a match to happen. The T before HA and the T after HA are both optional:

```
$ echo THAT | sed -r s/T?HAT?/++/
++
$ echo HA | sed -r s/T?HAT?/++/
++
```

Here are more examples to show how '\?' works. In each case, s replaces 'T\?HAT\?' with '++':

```
$ echo WHAT | sed -r s/T?HAT?/++/
W++
$ echo THAW | sed -r s/T?HAT?/++/
++W
```

WHAT and THAW show the matching parts. \? is 'greedy'. Given the choice of matching HA or HAT in WHAT, it chose HAT, to expand the extent of the match.

'as\?' matches 'a' or 'as':

```
$ echo am as | sed 's/as\?/=/g'
=m =
```

'b\?' matches 'nothing' or 'b':

```
$ echo '' | sed 's/b\?/=/'
=
$ echo bb | sed 's/b\?/=/'
=b
```

55

Chapter 6

* \+ \? Compared

It is important to memorize the difference between simple repetition Meta-Chars:

```
*     0 or more of previous
\+    1 or more of previous
\?    0 or 1 of previous
```

Matching 'zero occurrences' can be confusing at first. Some might say '\+' (1 or more) makes more 'sense' than '*' (0 or more). Actually, '*' tends to be used more.

It is best to just understand how '*', '\?' and '\+' behave. Then you will know what to expect. Here are some examples to compare how they work:

```
$ echo abc | sed 's/b*/=/'
=abc
$ echo abc | sed 's/b\?/=/'
=abc
```

- Both 'b*' and 'b\?' match 'nothing'.
- In both cases, 'nothing' changed to '='.

```
$ echo abbc | sed 's/b*/=/'
=abbc
$ echo abbc | sed 's/b\+/=/'
a=c
```

- 'b*' matches 'nothing'. Changed to '='.
- 'b\+' matches 'bb'. Changed to '='.

Simple Repetition MetaChars

```
$ echo abbbc | sed 's/ab\+/=/'
=c
$ echo abbbc | sed 's/ab\?/=/'
=bbc
```

- 'ab\+' matches 'abbb'. Changed to '='.
- 'ab\?' matches 'ab'. Changed to '='.

```
$ sed 's/[0-9]\+/X/' rgb
lower (#X): "red green blue"
UPPER (#X): "RED GREEN BLUE"
```

- '[0-9]\+' matches '1' and '2'.
- Both times, changed to 'X'.

```
$ sed 's/[0-9]*/=/' rgb
=lower (#1): "red green blue"
=UPPER (#2): "RED GREEN BLUE"
```

- '[0-9]*' matches 'nothing'.
- Both times, changed to '='.

```
$ sed 's/[0-9][0-9]*/=/' rgb
lower (#=): "red green blue"
UPPER (#=): "RED GREEN BLUE"
```

- '[0-9][0-9]*' matches '1' and '2'.
- Both times, changed to '='.

7: General Repetition MetaChars

Repetition MetaChars specify how many times the preceding character, character set, or grouping is repeated. As mentioned in the previous chapter, there are two categories of repetition MetaChars:

```
Simple:    *  \+  \?

General:   \{N\} \{L,\} \{L,H\}
```

This chapter explains the general ones (see previous chapter for the simple ones). Here are the general repetition MetaChars:

```
\{N\}      Exact N of Previous
\{L,\}     Low, Higher Previous
\{L,H\}    Low, High of Previous
```

\{N\} (Exact N of Previous)

'\{N\}' means N (a number) of the preceding character, character set, or group. For example, 'x\{3\}' exactly means 'xxx'.

```
            Matches
b\{4\}      bbbb
ab\{3\}c    abbbc
[0-9]\{2\}  00, ..., 99
```

General Repetition MetaChars

'bb' in abbc matches either b\{2\} or bb:

```
$ echo abbc | sed -r 's/b{2}/=/'
a=c
$ echo abbc | sed -r 's/bb/=/'
a=c
```

'bb' in abbc does not match b\{3\} or bbb:

```
$ echo abbc | sed -r 's/b{3}/=/'
abbc
$ echo abbc | sed -r 's/bbb/=/'
abbc
```

For low repetitions, either 'b\{4\}' or 'bbbb' is OK. For high repetitions, such as 'b\{33\}', it is obviously better to use the 'b\{33\}' version.

When would you use something like 'b\{33\}', or more realistically '.\{33\}'? It depends on your particular needs. It can certainly be useful for columnar data files.

\{L,\} (Low, Higher of Previous)

'\{L,\}' means L (low) to any higher number of the preceding character, character set, or group. For example, 'x\{2,\}' means xx, xxx, etc.

So b\{2,\} matches bb, bbb, bbbb, etc. Keeping in mind that repetition MetaChars are 'greedy', here are some examples:

```
$ echo abc | sed -r 's/b{2,}/#/'
abc
$ echo abbc | sed -r 's/b{2,}/#/'
a#c
$ echo abbbc | sed -r 's/b{2,}/#/'
a#c
```

59

Chapter 7

* (0 or more) is the same as '\{0,\}'. So bb in 'abbc' matches either 'bb*' or 'bb\{0,\}':

```
$ echo abbc | sed 's/bb*/=/'
a=c
$ echo abbc | sed 's/bb\{0,\}/=/'
a=c
```

The simple * is preferred to \{0,\}.

'\+' is the same as '\{1,\}'. So 'bb' in 'abbc' matches 'bb\+' or 'bb\{1,\}':

```
$ echo abbc | sed 's/bb\+/=/'
a=c
$ echo abbc | sed 's/bb\{1,\}/=/'
a=c
```

'\+' is much shorter. '\{1,\}' is perhaps more memorable.

\{L,H\} (Low, High of Previous)

'\{L,H\}' means L (low) to H (high) of the preceding character, character set, or group. For example, 'x\{3,4\}' means 'xxx' or 'xxxx'. L must be <= H.

```
                Matches
b\{2,3\}        bb, bbb
ab\{3,4\}c      abbbc, abbbbc
[0-9]\{2,3\}    00, ..., 999
```

60

'b\{2,3\}' matches bb or bbb:

```
$ echo abc | sed 's!b\{2,3\}!=!'
abc
$ echo abbc | sed 's!b\{2,3\}!=!'
a=c
$ echo abbbc | sed 's!b\{2,3\}!=!'
a=c
```

'\?' is the same as '\{0,1\}'. So 'bb' in 'abbc' matches 'bb\?' or 'bb\{0,1\}':

```
$ echo abbc | sed 's/bb\?/=/'
a=c
$ echo abbc | sed 's!bb\{0,1\}!=!'
a=c
```

'\?' is much shorter. '\{0,1\}' is perhaps more memorable.

The following table reinforces how each simple repetition MetaChar is a special case of a general repetition MetaChar:

```
a*      a\{0,\}     0 or more 'a'
a\+     a\{1,\}     1 or more 'a'
a\?     a\{0,1\}    0 or 1 'a'
```

8: Other RegEx MetaChars

This chapter covers the remaining RegEx MetaChars. MetaChars in this chapter are 'special cases', that did not fit within the previous chapters:

```
\|         Alternative Patterns
\( \)      Grouping and Saving
\`         Always Start of PatSpace
\'         Always End of PatSpace
```

\| (Alternative Patterns)

'\|' allows a match with one of several alternatives. For example, to change either 'red' or 'BLUE' to 'xxx':

```
$ sed "s/red\|BLUE/xxx/" rgb
lower (#1): "xxx green blue"
UPPER (#2): "RED GREEN xxx"
```

If the -r option is used, the '\|' MetaChar is written as '|' (clearer syntax):

```
$ sed -r "s/red|BLUE/xxx/" rgb
lower (#1): "xxx green blue"
UPPER (#2): "RED GREEN xxx"
```

'\|' regular expressions can be more complex. For example, to change 'g..' or 'B..' to 'xxx'.

```
$ sed -r "s/g..|B../xxx/g" rgb
lower (#1): "red xxxen blue"
UPPER (#2): "RED GREEN xxxE"
```

\(\) (Grouping and Saving)

\(and \) define a 'group' in a sed RegEx. The group is saved. Later, the group may be 'played back', using the BackRef MetaChar: \1, \2, etc.

To define a group, use both \(and \). Like \{ and \}, \(and \) are always used in pairs.

If the -r option is used, the \(and \) MetaChars are written (and) instead. Thus, the following forms have the same effect:

```
sed 's/\(.\) \(.\)/\2 \1/'
sed 's:\(.\) \(.\):\2 \1:'
```

```
sed -r 's/(.) (.)/\2 \1/'
sed -r 's:(.) (.):\2 \1:'
```

The first two forms are more cluttered, and headache-producing, because there are so many '\' characters. The second two forms, with the -r option, are easier to read.

Chapter 8

Here is an example using \(\) to reverse order:

```
$ echo xy|sed -r 's/(.)(.)/\2\1/'
yx
```

The RegEx '(.)(.)' matches 'xy'. So:

- Save 'x' and 'y' as groups.
- Play back groups, in reverse order ('yx').

Besides being saved and played back, groups may also be used with repetition MetaChars.

```
\(RegEx\)*     0 or more RegEx
\(RegEx\)\+    1 or more RegEx
\(RegEx\)\?    0 or 1 of RegEx
```

The following examples change an even number of 'A' characters (one or more 'AA') to '=':

```
$ cat AA.sed
s:\(AA\)\+:=:
```

```
$ echo A | sed -f AA.sed
A
```

```
$ echo AA | sed -f AA.sed
=
```

Other RegEx MetaChars

```
$ echo AAA | sed -f AA.sed
=A
```

```
$ echo AAAA | sed -f AA.sed
=
```

\` (Always Start of PatSpace)

If an Address (Chapter 10) uses the M modifier (/^A/M) or the s command uses the m flag (s/^A/B/m) (multi-line mode), ^ changes meaning to also match the empty string after a newline.

\` (BackSlash BackQuote) always matches 'start of PatSpace', whether multi-line mode or not. \` is rarely used, and is an advanced MetaChar.

\' (Always End of PatSpace)

If an Address uses the M modifier ('/A$/M') or the s command uses the m flag ('s/A$/B/m') (multi-line mode), $ changes meaning to also match the empty string before a newline.

\' (BackSlash SingleQuote) always matches 'end of PatSpace', whether multi-line mode or not. \' is rarely used, and is an advanced MetaChar.

If you really need to understand \` and \', in each example below, N appends the second line of input, so that PatSpace is '1\n2'.

Chapter 8

```
$ seq 2 | sed 'N; s/1$/=/m'
=
2
```

The example above, using the m flag, triggers multi-line mode, so '1$' matches '1' in '1\n2'.

```
$ seq 2 | sed 'N; s/1$/=/'
1
2
```

This second example does **not** use the m flag. So multi-line mode is not used, and '1$' does not match within '1\n2'.

```
$ seq 2 | sed "N; s/1\'/=/m"
1
2
```

1\' does not match within '1\n2', whether the m flag is used or not. We used "double quotes" because of the \' character.

9: SubEx MetaChars

SubEx = 'Substitution Expression'. SubEx is a replacement pattern, using Literals and MetaChars. In 's/A/B/', 'B' is the SubEx. s replaces the first matching portion of PatSpace with SubEx.

Examples of Literals in SubEx are 'new', 'B', and '\n' (newline). For example, 's/Z$/Z\n/' adds a new line after any line ending with Z.

In addition to hard-wired Literal characters in SubEx, sed allows you to use flexible MetaChars, explained in this chapter:

```
&    \1 \2 \3 ...  \9
\l \u \L \U \E
```

& (Entire Matched Portion)

In a SubEx, '&' substitutes (inserts) the entire matched portion of PatSpace.

```
$ seq 3 | sed 's/./Line &/'
Line 1
Line 2
Line 3
```

```
$ sed 's/...../[&]/' rgb
[lower] (#1): "red green blue"
[UPPER] (#2): "RED GREEN BLUE"
```

67

Chapter 9

Use '\&' to include a Literal ampersand (or '\\' to include a Literal Back-Slash) in the SubEx.

```
$ sed 's/...../[\&]/' rgb
[&] (#1): "red green blue"
[&] (#2): "RED GREEN BLUE"
```

\N BackRef (Play Saved Group)

To explain BackRef, it is easiest to start with an example, which reverses xy to yx:

```
$ echo xy|sed -r 's/(.)(.)/\2\1/'
yx
```

- '.' is a wildcard for any character.
- So '(.)(.)' matches 'xy' PatSpace.
- 'x' is stored in \1 BackRef.
- 'y' is stored in \2 BackRef.
- s replaces PatSpace with '\2\1' SubEx.

Each BackRef, such as \1 and \2, 'plays back' the contents of a saved group. In the example, \2 plays back y, \1 plays back x.

BackRef is mainly used with the s command. BackRef always looks like \1, \2, etc., up to \9.

BackRef is always used in combination with a \(\) group. BackRef refers back to what \(\) saved.

If \(\) is omitted, or there are not enough saved groups, BackRef is meaningless and results in an error. So 's/red/\1/' would result in an error.

68

Here is another example of BackRef, which changes xy to ax:

```
$ echo xy | sed -r 's/(.)./a\1/'
ax
```

- '.' is a wildcard for any character.
- So '(.).' matches 'xy' PatSpace.
- 'x' is stored in \1 BackRef.
- s replaces PatSpace with 'a\1' SubEx.

———

A BackRef may also be part of a RegEx. For example, '\([a-z]\)\1' matches aa, bb, cc, etc. Here is an example where BackRef matches a repeated character:

```
$ echo xx | sed -r 's/(.)\1/\1/'
x
```

- 'x' and 'x' are the same.
- So '(.)\1' matches 'xx' PatSpace.
- 'x' is stored in \1 BackRef.
- s replaces PatSpace with \1 SubEx.

———

In contrast:

```
$ echo xy | sed -r 's/(.)\1/\1/'
xy
```

- 'x' and 'y' are different.
- So '(.)\1' does not match 'xy'.
- So s does not do replacement.

Chapter 9

\l \u (Case for Next Character)

In a SubEx, '\l' changes the next character to lowercase; '\u' changes the next character to uppercase. Here are some examples:

```
$ cat rgb
lower (#1): "red green blue"
UPPER (#2): "RED GREEN BLUE"
```

```
$ sed 's/./\u&/g' rgb
LOWER (#1): "RED GREEN BLUE"
UPPER (#2): "RED GREEN BLUE"
```

- Line #1 is read into PatSpace.
- '.' is a wildcard for any character.
- s replaces each with '\u&' SubEx.
- AutoPrint PatSpace.

- Line #2 is read into PatSpace.
- Same steps happen as with line #1.

```
$ sed 's/w../\u&/' rgb
loWer (#1): "red green blue"
UPPER (#2): "RED GREEN BLUE"
```

- Line #1 is read into PatSpace.
- 'w..' matches 'wer'.
- s replaces with '\u&' SubEx.
- AutoPrint PatSpace.

- Line #2 is read into PatSpace.
- 'w..' is not found in PatSpace.
- AutoPrint PatSpace.

\L \U \E (Case for Next Span)

In a SubEx, '\L' changes the rest of SubEx to lowercase, until the next '\U' or '\E'. '\U' changes the rest of SubEx to uppercase, until the next '\L' or '\E'. Here are some examples:

```
$ sed 's/g../\U&/g' rgb
lower (#1): "red GREen blue"
UPPER (#2): "RED GREEN BLUE"
```

- Line #1 is read into PatSpace.
- 'g..' RegEx matches 'gre'.
- s replaces with '\U&' SubEx.
- AutoPrint PatSpace.

- Line #2 is read into PatSpace.
- 'g..' RegEx is not found in PatSpace.
- So s does not do any replacement.
- AutoPrint PatSpace.

```
$ sed 's/..[du]/\U&/g' rgb
lower (#1): "RED green BLUe"
UPPER (#2): "RED GREEN BLUE"
```

- Line #1 is read into PatSpace.
- '..[du]' RegEx matches 'red' and 'blu'.
- s replaces each with '\U&' SubEx.
- AutoPrint PatSpace.

- Line #2 is read into PatSpace.
- '..[du]' is not found in PatSpace.
- AutoPrint PatSpace.

Chapter 9

Note the difference if the previous example is changed to use \u (next letter uppercase):

```
$ sed 's/..[du]/\u&/g' rgb
lower (#1): "Red green Blue"
UPPER (#2): "RED GREEN BLUE"
```

Here is an example with \E (ends \L or \U):

```
$ cat UE.sed
# \1 - Word #1 -> Upper
# \2 - Word #2 -> no change
# \3 - Rest of line -> Lower
s!(\w+) (\w+) (.+)!\U\1\E \2 \L\3!
```

```
$ sed -r -f UE.sed rgb
lower (#1): "RED green blue"
UPPER (#2): "RED GREEN blue"
```

- Line #1 is read into PatSpace.
- '(\w+) (\w+)' matches 'red green'.
- '\3' stores the rest of the line ('.+').
- s replaces PatSpace with '\U\1\E \2 \L\3'.

- Line #2 is read into PatSpace.
- '(\w+) (\w+)' matches 'RED GREEN'.
- \3 stores the rest of the line (.+).
- s replaces PatSpace with '\U\1\E \2 \L\3'.

Why does not the first \w+ match 'lower'? It does, but '\w+ \w+' does not match 'lower (#1)'. The RegEx does not match until 'red green blue'.

This is the end of the chapters covering RegEx and SubEx. At this point, you know the s command, MetaChars, RegEx, and SubEx. The next chapter explains 'Addresses', to specify when the s command (or other sed command) runs.

10: Command Addresses

Each sed command takes an optional 'Address'. The 'Address' is a special syntax that comes immediately before the command.

If you do not use an Address, the command **always** runs. Using an Address lets you set when the command runs. Here are some Address examples:

```
     2 d         /[a-z]99/ d
     $ d            /[13]/ d
     $!d            /Ford/ d
   1,6 d       /Ford/,+22 d
   1~2 d        /aa/,/bb/ d
   3,$ d        /aa/,/bb/! d
   1,6! d         /xyz/,~5 d
   1~2! d         2,/xyz/ d
```

Addresses and commands go together. You cannot learn Addresses without using commands. You already know the s command. But s is not convenient to use for learning Addresses.

Instead, we will use the simple d command (Chapter 11) to help explain Addresses. d ('delete') deletes PatSpace, ends the sed script, reads the next input line into PatSpace, and restarts the script.

'[a1[,a2]][!]d' is the full syntax for the d command. '[a1,a2]]' is the Address. The Address is optional, as indicated by the [brackets]. The optional trailing '!' tells sed to invert the sense of Address matching.

'[a1[,a2]]' can be the following cases:

- Omitted (no Address)
- 'a1' (single Address)
- 'a1,a2' (Address range)

In addition, the Address can be one of the less commonly used special cases (explained below): 'a1,+N', 'a1,~N', and 'First~Step'.

Chapter 10

Address Omitted

If no Address, the command always runs.

```
$ seq 4 | sed 'd'
```

- Each line (1 2 3 4) is read into PatSpace.
- The d command is run on each line.
- Each line is deleted, so no output.

N Format Address

An 'N Format' Address runs the sed command on line N, based on sed's internal line counter. So 1d (or '1 d') runs d on line #1:

```
$ seq 4 | sed '1 d'
2
3
4
```

- Line #1 matches Address '1'.
- So d is run. PatSpace is cleared.
- Lines 2-4 do **not** match Address.
- So d is not run. AutoPrint PatSpace.

$ is a special N value that runs the sed command on the last input line. In the next example, the last line (no matter what the content) is deleted:

```
$ seq 4 | sed '$d'
1
2
3
```

Command Addresses

- Lines 1-3 are each read into PatSpace.
- None are the last line, so d not run.
- Line #4 (last) matches '$' Address.
- So d is run, and nothing is printed.

Note: sed "$d" will **not** work as desired, because the Unix shell interprets $d as a shell variable (Chapter 19). In contrast, sed '$d' protects $d from being interpreted by the shell.

L,H Format Address

An 'L,H' Address (low, high) runs the sed command on a range of lines. So '1,6 d' deletes lines 1-6:

```
$ seq 8 | sed '1,6 d'
7
8
```

- Lines 1-6 are each read into PatSpace.
- Each matches '1,6' Address, so d runs.
- Lines 7-8 are each read into PatSpace.
- '1,6' Address **not** matched, so d not run.

In an Address, $ means 'last line'. So 3,$ means lines 3, 4, ..., up to and including the final line:

```
$ seq 9 | sed '3,$ d'
1
2
```

- Lines 1-2 are each read into PatSpace.
- '3,$' Address **not** matched, so d not run.
- Lines 3-9 are each read into PatSpace.
- Each matches '3,$' Address, so d runs.

L (low) in L,H should normally be smaller than H (high). L <= H is expected. If L > H, only L matches:

```
$ seq 4 | sed '3,1 d'
1
2
4
```

- '3' (L) is bigger than '1' (H).
- So only '3' is used as the Address.

/RegEx/ Format Address

A '/RegEx/' Address runs the sed command when RegEx matches all or part of PatSpace. So '/red/ d' runs d when PatSpace contains 'red':

```
$ sed '/red/ d' rgb
UPPER (#2): "RED GREEN BLUE"
```

- First line contains '/red/' match.
- So d is run, and nothing is printed.
- Second line does not contain match.
- So d is not run. AutoPrint PatSpace.

Here is another example of using a '/RegEx/' Address (Recall that [13] matches 1 or 3):

```
$ seq 4 | sed '/[13]/ d'
2
4
```

- Lines 1 and 3 match '/[13]/' RegEx.
- So d is run, and nothing is printed.
- Lines 2 and 4 do not match RegEx.
- So d is not run. AutoPrint PatSpace.

Command Addresses

As shown below, '/[13]/' can be written to use another character instead of '/'. The following alternate forms are equivalent to the '/[13]/' form.

```
\![13]!     \.[13].
\#[13]#     \_[13]_
```

This can be used to avoid the unsightly 'Leaning Toothpick' appearance, when the RegEx has a directory path:

```
/\/a\/b\/c\/d\//   Harder to Read
\./a/b/c/d/.       Easier to Read
```

/red/I ('capital eye') makes /red/ case-insensitive. /red/I matches red, Red, RED, etc. So the first case only deletes the line with 'red'. The second case also deletes the line with 'RED':

```
$ sed '/red/ d' rgb
UPPER (#2): "RED GREEN BLUE"
```

```
$ sed '/red/I d' rgb
```

/^Red/M (Multi-line) makes ^ change meaning to also match the empty string **after** a newline. /^Red/ matches 'Red', but **not** 'X\nRed'. In contrast, /^Red/M matches both 'X\nRed' and 'Red'.

/Red$/M (Multi-line) makes $ change meaning to also match the empty string **before** a newline. /Red$/ matches 'Red', but **not** 'Red\nX'. In contrast, /Red$/M matches both 'Red\nX' and 'Red'.

If the above two paragraphs are not clear, please move on to the next section. The M multi-line option is advanced, and rarely used.

Chapter 10

/RegEx/,/RegEx/ Address

A '/RegEx/,/RegEx/' Address runs the sed command over a range of lines. For example, '/a/,/g/ d' runs d starting with the first line matching /a/, and ending with the first line matching /g/:

```
$ sed '/a/,/g/ d' a-i.txt
h
i
```

- First line (a) matches '/a/' RegEx.
- So d is run, and nothing is printed.
- Range continues until line matches '/g/'.
- Last 2 lines are after '/a/,/g/' range.
- So d is not run for the last two lines.

If the second RegEx never matches PatSpace, the command runs for all lines starting with the first matching line:

```
$ sed '/c/,/=/ d' a-i.txt
a
b
```

- Lines 1 and 2 do not match '/c/'.
- So d is not run for lines 1-2.
- Line #3 matches '/c/'. So d is run.
- No following lines match '/=/'.
- So d is run on remaining lines.

If the range occurs multiple times in the input, the command will be run for the range multiple times:

```
$ cat abcab.txt
a
b
c
a
b
```

Command Addresses

```
$ cat abcab.txt | sed '/a/,/b/ d'
c
```

- Both '/a/,/b/' ranges are deleted.
- 'c' line is between the ranges.

L,/RegEx/ Format Address

'L,/RegEx/' runs the command for a range of lines, starting at line L (Low), and ending at the next line where RegEx matches part of PatSpace.

For example, '1,/g/ d' runs d starting at line #1. Assuming enough input lines, d is run for at least two lines, until (and including) the next line matching /g/:

```
$ sed '1,/g/ d' a-i.txt
h
i
```

- First line matches '1' RegEx.
- So d is run, and nothing is printed.
- Range continues until line matches '/g/'.

♦ Last 2 lines are after '1,/g/' range.
♦ So d not run for last 2 lines (h and i).

---

sed "remembers" the status of a range between each Cycle. This is illustrated by the following variation on the previous example:

```
$ sed '1,/[gh]/ d' a-i.txt
h
i
```

If sed did not remember the range status, it might delete the line with 'h'. It might say: "Looks like we are in the '1,/[gh]/' range, so run d".

But the line with 'h' is not deleted. On the line with 'g', it says and remembers: "End of range, so from now on, d will **not** run, **unless** the line number is reset to 1".

Chapter 10

If the RegEx in 'L,/RegEx/' never matches PatSpace, the command is run for all lines starting with line L:

```
$ sed '3,/=/ d' a-i.txt
a
b
```

- Lines 1-2 are not line #3. So d not run.
- d is run on line #3, first line in range.
- No following lines match '/=/'.
- So d is run on remaining lines.

There is no line #0 in sed, so 0d is an error. But '0,/RegEx/' (a GNU extension) is a special Address range that allows one-line ranges.

'1,/RegEx/' starts the range at line #1, and starts looking for the end of the range (RegEx match) with line #2.

'0,/RegEx/' also starts the range at line #1 (no line #0 in sed), but starts looking for the end of the range (RegEx match) with line #1.

```
$ seq 3 | sed '1,/1/ d'
```

- Address range starts with line #1.
- Starting with line #2, '/1/' does not match.
- So Address range is not ended.
- So d is run for all lines.

```
$ seq 3 | sed '0,/1/ d'
2
3
```

- Address range starts with line #1.
- Uses special '0,/RegEx/' Address.
- '/1/' matches line #1, ending range.
- So d is only run for line #1.

/RegEx/,+N Format Address

A '/RegEx/,+N' Address (a GNU extension) runs the sed command if PatSpace contains RegEx, plus on the next N lines.

For example, '/b/,+5 d' runs d, starting at the first line where PatSpace matches '/b/', and continuing for the next 5 lines:

```
$ sed '/b/,+5 d' a-i.txt
a
h
i
```

- First line (a) does not match '/b/'.
- So d is not run. AutoPrint PatSpace.

- Second line (b) matches '/b/'.
- So d is run, and nothing is printed.
- Next 5 lines match '/b/,+5' Address.
- So d is run, and nothing is printed.

- Last 2 lines (h and i) do not match '/b/'.
- So d is not run. AutoPrint PatSpace.

Chapter 10

```
$ seq 14 | sed '/2/,+7 d'
1
10
11
```

- First line (1) does not match '/2/'.
- So d is not run. AutoPrint PatSpace.

- Line #2 matches /2/ RegEx.
- So d is run, and nothing is printed.
- Next 7 lines match '/2/,+7' Address.
- So d is run, and nothing is printed.

- Lines 10 and 11 do not match '/2/'.
- So d is not run. AutoPrint PatSpace.

- Line #12 matches '/2/' RegEx.
- So d is run, and nothing is printed.
- Remaining lines match '/2/,+7' Address.
- So d is run, and nothing is printed.

An 'N,+N' Address is also allowed, as in '1,+5' (Line #1 and following 5 lines). It is personal preference whether to use '1,+5' or the equivalent '1,6' format.

/RegEx/,~N Format Address

A '/RegEx/,~N' Address (a GNU extension) runs the sed command if PatSpace contains RegEx, and also on lines up to the next line that is a multiple of N.

For example, '/b/,~8 d' runs d, starting at the first line where PatSpace matches '/b/', and continuing up to line #8 (a multiple of 8).

```
$ sed '/b/,~8 d' a-i.txt
a
i
```

Command Addresses

- First line (a) does not match '/b/'.
- So d is not run. AutoPrint PatSpace.

♦ Second line (b) matches '/b/'.
♦ So d is run, and nothing is printed.
♦ Next 6 lines match '/b/,~8' Address.
♦ So d is run, and nothing is printed.

- Last line does not match '/b/'.
- So d is not run. AutoPrint PatSpace.

First~Step Address

A 'First~Step' Address (a GNU extension) runs the sed command on the 'First' line, the 'First + Step' line, the 'First + Step + Step' line, etc.

For example, '1~2 d' runs d on odd-numbered lines (1, 3, 5, etc.):

```
$ seq 5 | sed '1~2 d'
2
4
```

- sed reads each line into PatSpace.
- Lines 1, 3, 5 (odd) are deleted.
- Lines 2, 4 (even) are not deleted.

The syntax is 'First~Step'. Using the 1~2 example, 'First' is 1, and 'Step' is 2 (1, 3, 5, ...). Here are some more examples:

1~3 matches every 3rd line (1, 4, 7, ...).
2~3 matches every 3rd line (2, 5, 8, ...).
3~3 matches every 3rd line (3, 6, 9, ...).
4~4 matches every 4th line (4, 8, 12, ...).

Run the a command (Chapter 12) to append 'xx', after lines 4, 8, 12, ... (lengthy output not shown):

```
$ seq 9 | sed '4~4a xx'
```

Chapter 10

Run the c command (Chapter 12) to change the line to 'xxx', on lines 1, 4, 7, etc.

```
$ seq 4 | sed '1~3c xxx'
xxx
2
3
xxx
```

! (Inverts Address Match)

A ! directly after the Address inverts the sense of matching. Here are some examples:

```
    3!    Is not line #3
    $!    Is not last line
  1,2!    Is not line 1-2
 /ZZ/!    ZZ not in PatSpace
```

```
$ seq 4 | sed '$!  d'
4
```

- '$!' matches any line **except** last line.
- For lines 1-3, '$!' matches, so d runs.
- Line #4 does not match '$!', so not deleted.

84

Command Addresses

Delete PatSpace if does (or does not) contain 'lower':

```
$ sed '/lower/ d' rgb
UPPER (#2): "RED GREEN BLUE"
```

```
$ sed '/lower/!  d' rgb
lower (#1): "red green blue"
```

Delete PatSpace if is (or is not) in range '1,2':

```
$ seq 4 | sed '1,2 d'
3
4
```

```
$ seq 4 | sed '1,2!  d'
1
2
```

Deletes PatSpace if **not** in '/h/,/i/' range:

```
$ sed '/h/,/i/!  d' a-i.txt
h
i
```

You already knew the s command, RegEx, and SubEx. This chapter covered Addresses. The next chapters (Chapters 11-18) cover the remaining sed commands.

11: Delete PatSpace Content - dD

d and D delete content from PatSpace.

```
    What is Deleted
d   Entire PatSpace
D   PatSpace Line #1
```

Besides deleting content from PatSpace, d and D also change the flow of the sed script. After deleting, both d and D skip subsequent commands (abort the script) and restart the script.

d always reads the next input line before restarting the script. If PatSpace is empty after deleting line #1, D also reads the next input line.

sed d Command (delete)

d ('delete') deletes PatSpace, ends the sed script, reads the next input line into PatSpace, and restarts the script. Following are some d examples:

```
$ seq 4 | sed '$!  d'
4
```

- '$!' matches any line **except** last line.
- For lines 1-3, '$!' matches, so d runs.
- Line #4 does not match '$!', so not deleted.

```
$ sed '/\<GREEN\>/ d' rgb
lower (#1): "red green blue"
```

- '\<GREEN\>' matches Word 'GREEN'.
- So d is run on line with 'GREEN'.

```
$ sed '/\<GRE\>/ d' rgb
lower (#1): "red green blue"
UPPER (#2): "RED GREEN BLUE"
```

- '\<GRE\>' (Word) does **not** match.
- So d is **not** run on either line.

```
$ sed '/\bGREEN\b/ d' rgb
lower (#1): "red green blue"
```

- '\bGREEN\b' matches Word 'GREEN'.
- So d is run on line with 'GREEN'.

```
$ sed '/\bGRE\b/ d' rgb
lower (#1): "red green blue"
UPPER (#2): "RED GREEN BLUE"
```

- '\bGRE\b' (Word) does **not** match.
- So d is **not** run on either line.

```
$ sed '/\Bgreen\B/ d' rgb
lower (#1): "red green blue"
UPPER (#2): "RED GREEN BLUE"
```

- '\Bgreen\B' does **not** match 'green'.
- So d is **not** run on either line.

Chapter 11

```
$ sed '/\bGRE\B/ d' rgb
lower (#1): "red green blue"
```

- '\bGRE\B' matches part of 'GREEN'.
- So Line with 'GREEN' is deleted.

```
$ seq 3 | sed 'N; l; d; p'
1\n2$
3
```

- Line #1 is read into PatSpace.
- N appends line #2 to PatSpace.
- l (ell) displays PatSpace (1\n2$).
- d deletes PatSpace, restarts script.

- ◆ Line #3 is read into PatSpace.
- ◆ N tries to read next line.
- ◆ No more input, so the script ends.
- ◆ PatSpace ('3') AutoPrints.

```
$ seq 4 | sed 'N; l; d; p'
1\n2$
3\n4$
```

- Line #1 is read into PatSpace.
- N appends line #2 to PatSpace.
- l (ell) displays PatSpace (1\n2$).
- d deletes PatSpace, restarts script.

- ◆ Line #3 is read into PatSpace.
- ◆ N appends line #4 to PatSpace.
- ◆ l (ell) displays PatSpace (3\n4$).
- ◆ d deletes PatSpace, restarts script.
- ◆ No more input, so sed exits.

sed D Command (Delete)

If no \n (newline) in PatSpace, D ('Delete') behaves the same as the d command. If \n **is** in PatSpace, D deletes PatSpace line #1, including the first \n, and restarts the sed script **without** reading the next line.

Here is an example of how D works:

```
seq 3 | sed 'N; l; D; p'
1\n2$
2\n3$
3
```

- Line #1 is read into PatSpace.
- N appends line #2 to PatSpace.
- l (ell) displays PatSpace (1\n2$).
- D deletes '1\n', restarts script.

- N appends line #3 to PatSpace.
- l (ell) displays PatSpace (2\n3$).
- D deletes '2\n', restarts script.

- No more input for N.
- So jump to end of script.
- AutoPrint PatSpace (3).

Why does D restart the sed script? Why not go to the next command, since there may still be content in PatSpace?

Recall that d always restarts the script. Lee McMahon, the creator of sed, used the memorable wording: "d also has the side effect that no further commands are attempted on the corpse of a deleted line". d makes a 'dead corpse', so the script restarts.

Given that d ('dead') always restarts the script, D must also always restart the script. If D restarted the script when only the 'dead corpse' remained, and did **not** restart the script when content was left, script execution would be unpredictable.

To help remember the distinction between the sometimes confusing d and D commands: D only deletes line #1 of PatSpace. D does **not** read the next line if there is still content in PatSpace. Otherwise, d and D are the same. Both restart the script.

12: Append, Insert, Change - aic

This chapter covers three related commands that add new text to the output stream:

```
a Txt    Append Txt after lines
i Txt    Insert Txt before lines
c Txt    Change lines to Txt
```

Each command has a similar syntax, and allows an optional preceding Address, such as '1 a Txt', '1,4 i Txt', or '/red/ c Txt'.

Another similarity: Their output is not turned off by the -n command line option.

A final similarity: They do not change the line count. So if two lines are appended after input line #5, the next input line is still #6.

sed a Command (append)

'a Txt' ('append') schedules 'Txt' for later output. 'Txt' is written to standard output, either 1) just before N or n command tries to get the next input line, or 2) at the end of the sed script (after any AutoPrint).

'a Txt' does **not** change PatSpace. Appended text cannot be edited by subsequent script commands.

―――

Recall that the file 'rgb' has 2 lines. To append 'zzz' after the last line (Address is $):

```
$ cat rgb
lower (#1): "red green blue"
UPPER (#2): "RED GREEN BLUE"
```

Append, Insert, Change - aic

```
$ sed '$ a zzz' rgb
lower (#1): "red green blue"
UPPER (#2): "RED GREEN BLUE"
zzz
```

To append 'zzz' after a line if PatSpace contains a match with 'red':

```
$ sed '/red/ a zzz' rgb
lower (#1): "red green blue"
zzz
UPPER (#2): "RED GREEN BLUE"
```

sed i Command (insert)

'i Txt' ('insert') immediately inserts 'Txt' before the current line. The inserted text cannot be changed by subsequent script commands.

To insert 'aaa' before line #1 (Address is 1):

```
$ sed '1 i aaa' rgb
aaa
lower (#1): "red green blue"
UPPER (#2): "RED GREEN BLUE"
```

To insert 'aaa' before a line if PatSpace contains a match with 'BLUE':

```
$ sed '/BLUE/ i aaa' rgb
lower (#1): "red green blue"
aaa
UPPER (#2): "RED GREEN BLUE"
```

Chapter 12

sed c Command (change)

'c Txt' ('change') deletes PatSpace, skips the rest of the sed script, prints 'Txt', and then restarts a Cycle by reading the next input line.

To change the first line of the input file (Address is 1) to 'xxx':

```
$ sed '1 c xxx' rgb
xxx
UPPER (#2): "RED GREEN BLUE"
```

To change the line to 'xxx' if PatSpace contains 'BLUE':

```
$ sed '/BLUE/ c xxx' rgb
lower (#1): "red green blue"
xxx
```

If the Address for c is a range, the entire range is deleted, but the new text is printed just once.

```
$ seq 2 | sed '1,2 c xxx'
xxx
```

In contrast, the new text for a and i is printed for each line in the matching range.

```
$ seq 2 | sed '1,2 a xxx'
1
xxx
2
xxx
```

aic Syntax Alternatives

Older versions of sed required "multi-line syntax" for a, i, and c commands. Multi-line syntax places the text to append, insert, or substitute on the next line, as shown below.

Multi-line syntax is still allowed, and there is leeway in formatting with blanks, so the following three forms are equivalent in GNU sed:

```
1i \           1 i Txt
Txt            1i Txt
```

One-line syntax (two examples to the right) seems simpler and more convenient. If using multi-line syntax (example to the left), to prevent an error message, do **not** put spaces after the '\'.

———

The new text to append, insert, or change may be more than one line. Each continuation line ends with '\'. To append 'txt_1' and 'txt_2' if PatSpace contains a match with 'red':

```
$ cat a1.sed
/red/ a txt_1\
txt_2
```

```
$ sed -f a1.sed rgb
lower (#1): "red green blue"
txt_1
txt_2
UPPER (#2): "RED GREEN BLUE"
```

———

Chapter 12

An alternate (and arguably clearer) way to append more than one line is as follows:

```
$ cat a2.sed
# Append 2 lines after 'red'
/red/ a txt_1
/red/ a txt_2
```

```
$ sed -f a2.sed rgb
lower (#1): "red green blue"
txt_1
txt_2
UPPER (#2): "RED GREEN BLUE"
```

Conveniently, GNU sed and other modern sed versions let you use \n (newline) to separate lines:

```
$ sed '/red/ a xxx\nyyy' rgb
lower (#1): "red green blue"
xxx
yyy
UPPER (#2): "RED GREEN BLUE"
```

Suppose you want the added text to start with a blank. In the following case, the blank (between '\' and 'txt') is printed.

```
$ sed '/RED/ c \ txt' rgb
lower (#1): "red green blue"
 txt
```

Append, Insert, Change - aic

Cannot Edit a, i, c Results

Appended, inserted, or changed text cannot be edited by later commands. This is best shown by some examples, editing the file 'rgb'.

```
$ cat rgb
lower (#1): "red green blue"
UPPER (#2): "RED GREEN BLUE"
```

The a command does not change PatSpace. So later commands never see the appended text. Thus, when a4.sed is run, appended 'abc' text is not changed:

```
$ cat a4.sed
/red/ a abc
s/BLUE/xxxx/
s/abc/XYZ/
```

```
$ sed -f a4.sed rgb
lower (#1): "red green blue"
abc
UPPER (#2): "RED GREEN xxxx"
```

If the a command modified PatSpace, 'abc' might get changed to 'XYZ'. But PatSpace was **not** modified, so 's/abc/XYZ/' does not run. Here is what actually happens:

- Read line #1 into PatSpace.
- Run '/red/ a abc'. Queues 'abc'.
- Skip 's/BLUE/xxxx/' (no match).
- Skip 's/abc/XYZ/' (no match).
- Print PatSpace. Append 'abc'.

♦ Read line #2 into PatSpace.
♦ Skip '/red/ a abc' (no match).
♦ s replaces BLUE with 'xxxx'.
♦ Skip 's/abc/XYZ/' (no match).
♦ Print PatSpace.

95

Chapter 12

The i command does not change PatSpace. It immediately prints the inserted line(s). So later commands cannot see the inserted text. Thus, when i1.sed is run, the inserted 'abc' is not changed:

```
$ cat i1.sed
/red/ i abc
s/BLUE/1234/
s/abc/XYZ/
```

```
$ sed -f i1.sed rgb
abc
lower (#1): "red green blue"
UPPER (#2): "RED GREEN 1234"
```

If the i command modified PatSpace, 'abc' might get changed to 'XYZ'. But PatSpace was **not** modified, so 's/abc/XYZ/' does not run. Here is what actually happens:

- Read line #1 into PatSpace.
- Run '/red/ i abc', to print 'abc'.
- Skip 's/BLUE/1234/' (no match).
- Skip 's/abc/XYZ/' (no match).
- Print PatSpace.

♦ Read line #2 into PatSpace.
♦ Skip '/red/ i abc' (no match).
♦ s replaces BLUE with '1234'.
♦ Skip 's/abc/XYZ/' (no match).
♦ Print modified PatSpace.

Append, Insert, Change - aic

c deletes PatSpace, outputs the new text, and aborts the sed script. So the new text cannot be modified by the script. Thus, when c1.sed is run, the new '+++' is not changed to 'XXX':

```
$ cat c1.sed
/red/ c +++
s/BLUE/aaaa/
s/+++/XXX/
```

```
$ sed -f c1.sed rgb
+++
UPPER (#2): "RED GREEN aaaa"
```

If c changed line #1 to '+++' and continued, '+++' might later get changed to 'XXX'. But c deletes line #1, prints '+++', and then aborts the sed script. So 's/+++/XXX/' does not run. Here is what actually happens:

- Read line #1 into PatSpace.
- Run '/red/ c +++', which:
- Deletes PatSpace. Prints '+++'.
- Skips remaining script commands.

♦ Read line #2 into PatSpace.
♦ Skip '/red/ c +++' (no match).
♦ s replaces 'BLUE' with 'aaaa'.
♦ Skip 's/+++/XXX/' (no match).
♦ Print modified PatSpace.

In summary, results from a, i, and c cannot be edited by later commands. a and i do not modify PatSpace. c deletes PatSpace, prints the new text, and aborts the sed script.

13: Print PatSpace - pP l

Several commands (p, P, l) print PatSpace.

```
    What is Printed
p   Entire PatSpace
P   PatSpace Line #1
l   Debugging Form (ell)
```

sed p Command (print)

p ('print') prints PatSpace to the output stream. Normally, PatSpace Auto-Prints when the sed script ends. p lets you print PatSpace at any point:

```
$ echo AA | sed 'p; s/AA/ZZ/'
AA
ZZ
```

- sed reads 'AA' into PatSpace.
- p prints 'AA' to output stream.
- s changes 'AA' to 'ZZ'.
- AutoPrint 'ZZ' at end of script.

In combination with the -n command line option, p can limit printing to certain lines, as in this example:

```
$ seq 9 | sed -n '/7/ p'
7
```

- p runs if PatSpace contains '7'.
- -n option stops default AutoPrint.

Print PatSpace - pP 1

p and -n are typically used in combination. Here is another example:

```
$ seq 9 | sed -n '2,3p'
2
3
```

- p prints lines in '2,3' Address range.
- -n option stops default AutoPrint.

sed P Command (Print)

P ('Print') prints PatSpace line #1, up to the first \n (newline). If no \n, P behaves the same as p (prints entire PatSpace).

Here is an example of the P command:

```
$ seq 3 | sed -n 'N; l; P'
1\n2$
1
```

- sed reads '1' into PatSpace.
- N appends '2' to PatSpace.
- l prints PatSpace diagnostic (1\n2).
- P prints PatSpace first line (1).
- -n option stops PatSpace AutoPrint.

♦ sed reads '3' into PatSpace.
♦ N cannot read next line, so sed exits.
♦ -n option stops AutoPrint of PatSpace.

Chapter 13

sed l Command (display line)

l ('list') displays PatSpace in a special format, such as '1\n2$', for debugging. l is not typically used for production scripts.

l takes an optional line-wrap parameter. 'l 70' (default unless changed by -l command line option) splits long lines at 70 characters. 'l 0' turns off line-wrap.

An example of how l (ell) might be used:

```
$ seq 3 | sed 'N; l; d; p'
1\n2$
3
```

- sed reads '1' into PatSpace.
- N appends next line to PatSpace.
- l displays PatSpace ('1\n2$').
- d deletes PatSpace, aborts script.

♦ sed reads '3' into PatSpace.
♦ N fails to read next line.
♦ So sed jumps to end of script.
♦ PatSpace ('3') AutoPrints.

The http://aurelio.net/sedsed/ utility, created by Aurelio Jargas, is another great way to do diagnostic testing. I used sedsed to help verify the logic for some of the examples in this book.

14: Read / Write File - rR wW

```
rR  Read from 'Rfile' to stdout
wW  Write from PatSpace to 'Wfile'
```

```
    Which Lines are Printed
rw  All Lines
RW  Next Line
```

```
    When Lines are Printed
rR  Later (Usually End of Script)
wW  Immediately
```

The r and R commands schedule lines from a separate file to be printed later.

- 'r Rfile' schedules **all** lines from Rfile.
- 'R Rfile' schedules **next** line from Rfile.
- r and R both print to standard output.

Similar to aic output (Chapter 12), the output from r and R is **not** suppressed by the -n command line option, and cannot be edited by subsequent sed script commands.

The w and W commands immediately write lines from PatSpace to a separate file.

- 'w Wfile' writes **all lines** to Wfile.
- 'W Wfile' writes **first line** to Wfile.
- w and W both write from PatSpace.

Chapter 14

sed r Command (read Rfile)

'r Rfile' ('read') schedules printing Rfile contents, either 1) just before N or n command tries to get the next input line, or 2) at the end of the sed script (after sed AutoPrints).

If Rfile cannot be read, r does nothing, and no error occurs. If Rfile is /dev/stdin, input is taken from standard input.

```
$ cat rgb
lower (#1): "red green blue"
UPPER (#2): "RED GREEN BLUE"
```

Recall that rgb has 2 lines, as above. Here are several examples showing the r command:

```
$ seq 2 | sed '1 r rgb'
1
lower (#1): "red green blue"
UPPER (#2): "RED GREEN BLUE"
2
```

- '1' is read into PatSpace.
- Address (1) matches, so r queues rgb.
- Script ends. '1' AutoPrints.
- Contents of rgb are printed.

♦ '2' is read into PatSpace.
♦ Address does not match, so r is not run.
♦ Script ends. '2' AutoPrints.

Read / Write File - rR wW

```
$ seq 2 | sed '1r /dev/stdin' rgb
lower (#1): "red green blue"
1
2
UPPER (#2): "RED GREEN BLUE"
```

- Line #1 is read into PatSpace.
- Address matches, so r queues stdin.
- Script ends. AutoPrint PatSpace.
- stdin contents ('1\n2') are printed.

♦ Line #2 is read into PatSpace.
♦ Address does not match, so r is not run.
♦ Script ends. AutoPrint PatSpace.

———

sed -e '/zzz/ r Rfile' -e '/zzz/ d' is a typical usage. The script reads in Rfile after any line including 'zzz', and then deletes the line with 'zzz'. (Note use of multiple -e command line options.)

sed R Command (Read Rfile)

'R Rfile' ('Read') schedules printing the next line from Rfile, either 1) just before N or n command tries to get the next input line, or 2) at the end of the sed script (after sed AutoPrints).

Each R invocation reads the next line from Rfile. The first time, line #1 is read, the second time, line #2, etc.

If Rfile cannot be read, or is at end of file, R does nothing, and no error occurs. If Rfile is /dev/stdin, input is taken from standard input.

———

```
$ cat rgb
lower (#1): "red green blue"
UPPER (#2): "RED GREEN BLUE"
```

The rgb file has 2 lines, as above. Here are several R command examples, with explanation for the first few examples:

———

Chapter 14

```
$ seq 2 | sed '/[12]/ R rgb'
1
lower (#1): "red green blue"
2
UPPER (#2): "RED GREEN BLUE"
```

- '1' is read into PatSpace.
- '1' matches '[12]', so R queues rgb.
- Script ends. '1' AutoPrints.
- Line #1 of rgb is printed.

- ◆ '2' is read into PatSpace.
- ◆ '2' matches '[12]', so R queues rgb.
- ◆ Script ends. '2' AutoPrints.
- ◆ Next line (#2) of rgb is printed.

———

```
$ seq 2 | sed '1R /dev/stdin' rgb
lower (#1): "red green blue"
1
UPPER (#2): "RED GREEN BLUE"
```

- Line #1 is read into PatSpace.
- Address matches, so R queues stdin.
- Script ends. AutoPrint PatSpace.
- Line #1 of stdin ('1') is printed.

- ◆ Line #2 is read into PatSpace.
- ◆ Address does not match, so R is not run.
- ◆ Script ends. AutoPrint PatSpace.

———

Read / Write File - rR wW

```
$ seq 3 | sed '/2/ R rgb'
1
2
lower (#1): "red green blue"
3
```

```
$ seq 3 | sed '1,2 R rgb'
1
lower (#1): "red green blue"
2
UPPER (#2): "RED GREEN BLUE"
3
```

```
$ seq 3 | sed '/2/,/3/ R rgb'
1
2
lower (#1): "red green blue"
3
UPPER (#2): "RED GREEN BLUE"
```

sed w Command (write Wfile)

'w Wfile' ('write') appends PatSpace to Wfile. Wfile is created (or truncated) at sed startup. If Wfile cannot be written, sed exits with an error. Wfile is kept open until sed exits.

- 'w /dev/stdout' writes PatSpace to stdout.
- 'w /dev/stderr' writes PatSpace to stderr.

Chapter 14

```
$ seq 2 | sed -n '1 w a.txt'
$ cat a.txt
1
```

The result is one line (1) in the a.txt file. The 'cat' command displays the file contents.

- '1' is read into PatSpace.
- Address matches, so w writes '1'.
- Uses -n, so '1' does not AutoPrint.

- '2' is read into PatSpace.
- Address does not match, so w not run.
- Uses -n, so '2' does not AutoPrint.

```
$ seq 2 | sed -n '/2/ w a.txt'
$ cat a.txt
2
```

```
$ seq 4 | sed -n '2,3 w a.txt'
$ cat a.txt
2
3
```

```
$ seq 8 | sed -n '/5/,/6/ w a.txt'
$ cat a.txt
5
6
```

```
$ seq 8 | sed -n '5,6w /dev/stdout'
5
6
```

In the last example, the lines are written to standard output, so they appear on the screen, not in a file.

———

Because 'p' and 'w /dev/stdout' both print PatSpace to standard output, the results from the following two commands are the same:

```
$ seq 9 | sed -n '8w /dev/stdout'
8
$ seq 9 | sed -n '8p'
8
```

sed W Command (Write Wfile)

'W Wfile' ('Write') appends line #1 of PatSpace (up to any first newline) to Wfile. W is a GNU extension.

Wfile is created (or truncated) at sed startup. If Wfile cannot be written, sed exits with an error. Wfile is kept open until sed exits.

- 'W /dev/stdout' writes line #1 to stdout.
- 'W /dev/stderr' writes line #2 to stderr.

Here are some W examples:

———

Chapter 14

```
$ seq 3 | sed -n 'N; 2 W a.txt'
$ cat a.txt
1
```

W is run on the second line of the input stream. The -n option stops default AutoPrint output.

- '1' is read into PatSpace.
- N appends '2' to PatSpace.
- W writes '1' to Wfile.
- -n option, so '1\n2' not printed.

♦ '3' is read into PatSpace.
♦ N tries to append next line.
♦ No next line, so script ends.
♦ -n option, so '3' not printed.

```
$ seq 4 | sed -n 'N; /2/,/3/W a.txt'
$ cat a.txt
1
3
```

The above example runs W on the line if PatSpace contains '2', up until the line where PatSpace contains '3'.

- '1' is read into PatSpace.
- N appends '2' to PatSpace.
- W writes '1' to a.txt file.
- -n option, so '1\n2' not printed.

♦ '3' is read into PatSpace.
♦ N appends '4' to PatSpace.
♦ W writes '3' to a.txt file.
♦ -n option, so '3\n4' not printed.

15: Read Line into PatSpace - nN

	n	N
Overwrite PatSpace	yes	-
Append to PatSpace	-	yes
Exit if Read Fails	yes	yes
Print Before Read	yes	-
Print Before Exit	-	yes

At the start of each Cycle, sed reads a line into PatSpace. Before the line is read into PatSpace, sed AutoPrints PatSpace, unless the -n command line option has been used.

The n and N commands read input into PatSpace at **any** point during a sed script, and increment sed's internal line counter.

sed n Command (next line)

n ('next') reads the next input line into PatSpace. n prints PatSpace before trying to read the line, unless the -n command line option is used.

The sed script normally continues after n runs. But if no more input for n to read, sed exits, without trying to print PatSpace again.

Chapter 15

Here is an example of how n works. (Note: As described in Chapter 15, bk branches to the :k Label.) The script prints the line **after** a matching line. First, we show the case where **not** adjacent matching lines:

```
$ cat pl-am.sed
/5/ {:k n; p; /5/ bk}
```

```
$ seq 9 | sed -n -f pl-am.sed
6
```

- Line #5 matches '/5/'. So { } runs.
- n reads next line (6) into PatSpace.
- p prints PatSpace (6).

♦ PatSpace (6) does not match '/5/'.
♦ So bk does not branch.

- No more output, because:
- -n option disabled AutoPrint, and
- { } only runs for line #5.

———

For the more complex case with adjacent matching lines (eg, 50, 51, 52 all contain '5'), b branches, n reads the next line, and p prints it:

```
$ seq 49 52 | sed -n -f pl-am.sed
51
52
```

sed N Command (Next Line)

N ('Next') appends the next input line to PatSpace, after a newline. The sed script normally continues after N runs. But if no more input for N to read, sed exits, after printing PatSpace (if -n command line option not used).

Here is an example of how N works:

```
seq 3 | sed 'N; l; D; p'
1\n2$
2\n3$
3
```

- Line #1 is read into PatSpace.
- N appends line #2 to PatSpace.
- l (ell) displays PatSpace (1\n2$).
- D deletes '1\n', restarts script.

- N appends line #3 to PatSpace.
- l (ell) displays PatSpace (2\n3$).
- D deletes '2\n', restarts script.

- No more input for N.
- So jump to end of script.
- AutoPrint PatSpace (3).

It is easy to get confused about n and N. To help you remember, here is the comparison again:

1) Both commands read the next line. 2) n overwrites, N appends. 3) n prints PatSpace before reading the next line. N does **not** print before reading.

```
                     n     N
Overwrite PatSpace   yes   -
Append to PatSpace   -     yes
Exit if Read Fails   yes   yes
Print Before Read    yes   -
Print Before Exit    -     yes
```

111

16: Access HoldSpace - hH gG x

HoldSpace is the sed secondary 'swap space'. You cannot directly edit the contents of HoldSpace. Instead, HoldSpace is used to temporarily hold or gather up the contents of PatSpace.

Only five sed commands ('hold', 'Hold', 'get', 'Get, 'exchange') use HoldSpace:

```
h: PatSpace  > HoldSpace (copy)
H: PatSpace >> HoldSpace (append)

g: HoldSpace  > PatSpace (copy)
G: HoldSpace >> PatSpace (append)

x: PatSpace <> HoldSpace (swap)
```

To help remember the commands:

- hH - **Hold to** HoldSpace from PatSpace.
- gG - **Get from** HoldSpace to PatSpace.

♦ GH - **Append to** destination (after \n).
♦ gh - **Copy to (overwrite)** destination.

Recall that PatSpace is cleared before a new input line is read, at the start of a Cycle. In contrast, HoldSpace is only modified if you specifically direct (with h, H, or x).

sed h Command (hold)

h ('hold') copies the contents of PatSpace to HoldSpace. The original contents of HoldSpace are overwritten.

sed H Command (Hold)

H ('Hold') **appends** the contents of PatSpace to HoldSpace, after a newline character. The original contents of HoldSpace are retained.

sed g Command (get)

g ('get') copies the contents of HoldSpace to PatSpace. The original contents of PatSpace are overwritten.

sed G Command (Get)

G ('Get') **appends** the contents of HoldSpace to PatSpace, after a newline character. The original contents of PatSpace are retained.

sed x Command (exchange)

x ('exchange') swaps the contents of PatSpace and HoldSpace. Any previous contents of PatSpace and HoldSpace are overwritten.

Chapter 16

Examples - HoldSpace (gGhHx)

```
$ cat rgb
lower (#1): "red green blue"
UPPER (#2): "RED GREEN BLUE"
```

Again, the 'rgb' file has 2 lines, as above. The following script prints the original version of a line, after any substituted version:

```
$ sed '/RED/{h; s//=/; p; x}' rgb
lower (#1): "red green blue"
UPPER (#2): "= GREEN BLUE"
UPPER (#2): "RED GREEN BLUE"
```

- Line #1 does not match 'RED'.
- So { } command group does not run.
- AutoPrint PatSpace.

- Line #2 matches 'RED', so { } runs.
- h holds line ('UPPER ...') to HoldSpace.
- s changes 'RED' to '='. p prints PatSpace.
- x exchanges HoldSpace and PatSpace.
- AutoPrint PatSpace at end of script.

'seq 9' prints 1 to 9, one per line. The example below prints the line before each matching line:

```
$ seq 9 | sed -n '/5/{g; 1!p}; h'
4
```

- -n suppresses AutoPrint.
- So only p produces output.

- Line #1 ('1') does not contain '5'.
- So { } command group does not run.
- h copies '1' to HoldSpace.

- Lines 2-4 and 6-9 have the same logic.
- After line #4, HoldSpace contains '4'.

Access HoldSpace - hH gG x

- Line #5 ('5') matches, so { g; 1!p } runs.
- g copies HoldSpace (4) to PatSpace.
- Line #5 is not #1 (1!), so p prints 4.

The following example reverses the lines in a file, printing the last line first:

```
$ seq 3 | sed '1!G; h; $!d'
3
2
1
```

- 1! means 'is not first line'.
- $! means 'is not last line'.

- Line #1 is read into PatSpace.
- 1!G is skipped, because line #1.
- h copies PatSpace ('1') to HoldSpace.
- $!d deletes PatSpace, starts new Cycle.

- Line #2 is read into PatSpace.
- 1!G appends HoldSpace to PatSpace.
- h copies PatSpace (2\n1) to HoldSpace.
- $!d deletes PatSpace, starts new Cycle.

- Line #3 is read into PatSpace.
- 1!G appends HoldSpace to PatSpace.
- h copies PatSpace (3\n2\n1) to HoldSpace.
- Skip $!d (last line). AutoPrint PatSpace.

17: Branch / Quit - : btT / qQ

sed is a very useful stream editor, a way to process and transform text. sed is **not** a real programming language, certainly not in the sense of C, python, JavaScript, etc.

Nevertheless, sed does have certain programming constructs. The b, t, and T commands branch to Labels, or to the end of the sed script. This lets sed somewhat emulate a programming language.

This chapter also covers two sed commands, q and Q, used to quit (totally branch out of) sed.

sed : (Label, eg :k)

A 'Label' is the destination for b, t, or T. So ':k' is the destination for 'b k' (or 'bk'). For one-line, simple scripts, keep Labels short.

:f, :j, :k, and :loop are four examples of typical Labels (using a letter not otherwise used in sed, or a short word).

It is an error to specify a Label (such as 'bk'), and not include :k (the destination) in the script.

A sed Label is not a sed command. It is a marker, a destination. So, for example, a Label does not take an Address.

It is easy to forget whether the colon comes before or after. Is it k: or :k syntax? It is :k of course.

Here is how to remember. Tell yourself it **has** to be :k because sed would get confused if the name came first. The colon tells sed 'This is a label', and then sed reads the following label text.

Ignore the fact that sed scripts are pre-compiled at sed start-up. To remember :k is the correct form, think 'colon **has** to come first, so sed knows it is a label, not some other sed command'.

sed b Command (branch)

b ('branch') branches to end of the sed script.
bk (or 'b k') branches to the :k Label.

sed t Command (test)

t ('test') branches to the end of the sed script if s replaced since the current line was read, or since the last t/T branch was taken.

tk (or 't k') applies the same test, but branches to the :k Label.

sed T Command (Test)

T ('Test') branches to the end of the sed script if s has **not** replaced since the current line was read, or since the last t/T branch was taken.

Tk (or 'T k') applies the same test, but branches to the :k Label.

Branching Examples

```
$ seq 3 | sed 's/2/=/; b; d'
1
=
3
```

- b always branches.
- So d never runs.
- 1 and 3 are printed.
- s changes line #2 to '='.

```
$ seq 3 | sed 's/2/=/; t; d'
=
```

- For lines 1 and 3, s does not run.
- So t does not branch, and d runs.
- s changes line #2 to '='.
- So t branches, d skipped, '=' prints.

Chapter 17

```
$ seq 3 | sed 's/2/=/; T; d'
1
3
```

- For lines 1 and 3, s does not run.
- So T branches, d skipped, line prints.
- s changes line #2 to '='.
- So T does not branch, and d is run.

```
$ seq 3 | sed 's/1/=/; bk; d; :k N'
=
2
3
```

- For line #1, s changes 1 to '='.
- bk branches to :k Label.
- N appends 2. AutoPrint '=\n2'.
- Line #3 AutoPrints (d skipped).

```
$ seq 3 | sed 's/1/=/; tk; d; :k N'
=
2
```

- s changes line #1 to '='. t branches.
- N appends '2'. AutoPrint '=\n2'.
- For line #3, s does not replace.
- So t does not branch, and d runs.

118

```
$ seq 3 | sed 's/1/=/; Tk; d; :k N'
2
3
```

- s changes line #1 to '='.
- So T does not branch, and d runs.
- For line #2, s fails, so T branches.
- N appends '3'. AutoPrint '2\n3'.

sed q Command (quit)

q ('quit') quits sed without processing more commands or input. PatSpace is printed (unless -n command line option). q takes a single Address, such as '9q', and an optional exit code, such as 'q3'.

```
$ seq 9 | sed '2q'
1
2
```

- Line #1 does not match 2 Address.
- AutoPrint PatSpace.
- Line #2 matches 2 Address.
- q exits script, AutoPrints, quits sed.

Chapter 17

sed Q Command (Quit)

Q ('Quit') quits sed without processing more commands or input. PatSpace is **not** printed. Q takes a single Address, such as '9Q', and an optional exit code, such as 'Q1'. Q is a GNU extension.

```
$ seq 9 | sed '2Q'
1
```

- Line #1 does not match 2 Address.
- AutoPrint PatSpace.
- Line #2 matches 2 Address.
- Q exits script, quits sed.

The only difference between q and Q is:

- q prints PatSpace if not -n option.
- Q never prints PatSpace.

18: Other Actions - { } # eyvz =

The following sed commands and syntax elements do not really fit into previous categories. Each is somewhat unique.

sed { } (grouping)

{ } ('group') defines a command group. If the Address for the group matches, commands in the group are run.

You may nest { } within another { } group. Also, a command within { } may use its own Address.

There is no point in using { } without an Address. A group only influences sed script behavior if the group has an Address.

Here is an example of { } used to insert a blank line above each matching line:

```
$ seq 2 | sed '/2/ {x; p; x}'
1

2
```

- sed reads '1' into PatSpace.
- '2' not found, so {x; p; x} not run.
- AutoPrint PatSpace (1).

♦ sed reads '2' into PatSpace.
♦ '2' matches, so {x; p; x} is run:

- x swaps PatSpace and HoldSpace.
- p prints PatSpace (blank line)
- x swaps PatSpace and HoldSpace.
- AutoPrint PatSpace (2).

Chapter 18

An alternative attempt, not using the { } syntax, does not work properly:

```
$ seq 2 | sed '/2/x; /2/p; /2/x'
1
```

- sed reads '1' into PatSpace.
- 2 not found, so x, p, and x do not run.
- AutoPrint PatSpace (1).

♦ sed reads '2' into PatSpace.
♦ '2' matches PatSpace, so x runs.
♦ x swaps PatSpace and HoldSpace.
♦ Now no match, so p and x not run.
♦ Empty AutoPrint PatSpace.

Below is a non-grouped alternative that also prints a blank line above each matching line:

```
$ seq 2 | sed '/2/x; /^$/p; /^$/x'
1

2
```

You may nest { } within another { } group. Also, a command within { } may use its own Address. This example shows these capabilities:

```
$ seq 3 | sed '1,2{x; p; 2{p}; x}'

1


2
3
```

122

- sed reads '1' into PatSpace.
- Is line #1, so '1,2{ ... }' is run:

♦ x swaps PatSpace and HoldSpace.
♦ p prints PatSpace (blank line).
♦ Is line #1, so '2{p}' does not run.
♦ x swaps PatSpace and HoldSpace.
♦ AutoPrint PatSpace (1).

- sed reads '2' into PatSpace.
- Is line #2, so '1,2{ ... }' is run:

♦ x swaps PatSpace and HoldSpace.
♦ p prints PatSpace (blank line)
♦ Is line #2, so '2{p}' prints blank line.
♦ x swaps PatSpace and HoldSpace.
♦ AutoPrint PatSpace (2).

- sed reads '3' into PatSpace.
- Is line #3, so '1,2{ ... }' not run.
- AutoPrint PatSpace (3).

sed # (comment marker)

All text after the # symbol, up to the end of the line, is a comment. This is useful for documenting sed scripts.

```
$ cat a2.sed
# Append 2 lines after 'red'
/red/ a txt_1
/red/ a txt_2
```

As a special case, #n at top of a sed script has the same effect as the -n command line option.

Chapter 18

sed e Command (execute)

e ('execute' or 'evaluate') executes the command in PatSpace, and replaces PatSpace with the output (minus the trailing newline).

'e command' executes 'command', and immediately prints any output to the output stream.

The e command is rarely used. In the following example, 'cmd' is set to 'uname -o', and the output is 'GNU/Linux'.

```
$ sed '1e uname -o' rgb
GNU/Linux
lower (#1): "red green blue"
UPPER (#2): "RED GREEN BLUE"
```

sed v Command (version)

v ('version') does nothing. v is related to script portability. Other versions of sed, that do **not** have the v command, fail when they encounter v.

Also, v takes an optional argument (default = 4.0) to specify the version of GNU sed the script requires. You will probably never use v.

sed y Command (transliterate)

y ('transliterate') transliterates source characters to destination characters. For example, 'y/ab/AB/' changes 'a' to 'A', 'b' to 'B'.

y is a poor substitute for the Unix 'tr' command, because y does not use character classes (such as '0-9' or [:alpha:]). For complex sed scripts, y is often necessary. But a more practical approach is usually to use short sed scripts from within a shell script, along with tr and other Unix commands.

Here is a simple example of the y command:

```
$ sed 'y/()/[]/' rgb
lower [#1]: "red green blue"
UPPER [#2]: "RED GREEN BLUE"
```

sed z Command (zap)

z ('zap') clears PatSpace. z is usually the same as 's/.*//'. However, 's/.*//' will fail if there are invalid multi-byte sequences in the input stream.

```
$ sed '/red/ z' rgb

UPPER (#2): "RED GREEN BLUE"
```

```
$ sed '/red/ s/.*//' rgb

UPPER (#2): "RED GREEN BLUE"
```

sed = Command (line #)

= ('line #') prints the line number for one or more lines, followed by a newline. The = command is not used much in sed scripts.

```
$ echo green | sed '='
1
green
```

- 'green' is read into PatSpace.
- = prints '1' to output stream.
- Script ends. 'green' AutoPrints.

Chapter 18

In these examples, -n suppresses AutoPrint, so the only output is from the = command:

```
$ seq 9 | sed -n '/4/ ='
4
```

```
$ seq 9 | sed -n '3,4 ='
3
4
```

```
$ seq 9 | sed -n '$ ='
9
```

19: General Advice about sed

This chapter covers general considerations and advice in using sed.

When to Use (or not Use) sed

There are no hard and fast rules concerning when and how to use sed. The advice and opinions in this section are based on my experience and the writings of others I have read.

sed is useful for doing short, discrete tasks, in combination with other Unix utilities. The most useful sed command, by far, is the s (substitute) command. sed works well with text files, shell scripts, and other Unix tools.

I typically use one-line sed scripts from within shell scripts, in combination with other Unix commands. Instead of trying to 'do everything' with an over-complex sed script, I use smaller steps that are easier to understand and verify.

A long sed script can be fine, if it is easy to understand and maintain. For example, to make many editing changes to many files, each editing change (in 's/A/B/' format) could be a single line in a long sed script.

Despite even being used to write games, sed is **not** a real programming language. For example, sed only weakly emulates functions (using branches and Labels). And sed does not have variables or arrays.

If the input data file has fields, it usually better to use awk. Also, awk does have functions, variables, and arrays, so can be used as a programming language.

If you want to do something more complex, it is better to use C, C++, C#, Java, Python, Perl, etc. Complex sed scripts can be confusing and hard to maintain, compared with code written in a real programming language.

Also, anytime you have a complex scripting task, it is a good idea, before jumping into writing a complex sed script, to first check if there is an existing Unix utility that does what you need, or might be used in combination with sed.

This book teaches a streamlined, compact way to use sed commands. Once you are familiar with sed, you will probably find other ways to use it, depending on your software environment and what you are trying to accomplish.

For example, I frequently call sed from within C programs. Perhaps few others do that. But I find it very useful for editing and importing data files. The C code provides the 'glue' to create and call the sed scripts.

I use sed on Unix computers, because Unix is my normal work environment for programming and data processing. But you can use sed on a Windows PC, if that is your preference. You are free to use sed in many different ways and environments.

Quoting Command-Line Scripts

Repeating and expanding upon information presented in Chapter 1, there are three different ways command-line sed scripts may be quoted:

```
1)   quotes omitted
2)   "double quotes"
3)   'single quotes'
```

For many simple sed scripts, the quoting makes no difference. For example, the following sed commands behave exactly the same way:

```
1) sed    s/old/new/    old.txt
2) sed   "s/old/new/"   old.txt
3) sed   's/old/new/'   old.txt
```

For simple command-line scripts with no blanks, you may use whichever quoting style you prefer. If unsure, use the 'single quote' version.

———

If there are blanks within a command-line sed script, and quotes are not used, there will definitely be a problem.

The following examples try to change 'A B' to 'Y Z'. The first produces an error message. Quotes are required because of the embedded blanks.

```
1) sed    s/A B/Y Z/      (Fails)
2) sed   "s/A B/Y Z/"     Works
3) sed   's/A B/Y Z/'     Works
```

The second two work as intended. Either 'single' or "double" quotes enclose the sed script. The shell (and sed) sees 's/A B/Y Z/' as one concept, instead of separate 's/A', 'B/Y' and 'Z/' items.

———

General Advice about sed

There are other times when it is required to use 'single quotes', so that certain special characters are not interpreted by the Unix shell.

$x indicates the shell variable 'x'. If no quotes, or "double quotes", the shell will interpret $x as a shell variable.

'Single quotes' prevent the shell from trying to interpret '$2', as shown here:

```
1) sed "s/$2/2 bucks/"
2) sed 's/$2/2 bucks/'
```

Example 1) fails. sed tries to interpret "$2" as a variable. The result is an error message.

Example 2) works. The single quotes protect '$2' from being interpreted (read as a shell variable).

If you are unsure, enclose command line scripts with 'single quotes'. This avoids problems with: 1) blanks, and 2) certain special characters.

Sometimes, you **want** sed to interpret $ as the start of a shell variable.

In that case, "double quotes" allow the sed script to work as intended. For example, here is a segment from a shell script:

```
x=YES           Set $x to YES.
sed "s/$x/N/"   Works OK.
sed 's/$x/N/'   Fails.  $x hidden.
```

x=YES sets the shell variable x to 'YES'.

sed command #1 surrounds the sed script with "double quotes", allowing the shell to use the shell variable.

sed command #2 runs, but not as intended. Instead of seeing '$x' as a variable, the shell sees '$x' as Literal characters.

Alternatively, a way to use double quotes and avoid conflict with the shell is to use "\$x". The BackSlash tells the shell to use the Literal '$'.

As you can probably tell, shell command line quoting can be a little tricky. Sometimes, you may need to experiment.

If the sed script is included within a separate file, and invoked with the sed -f option, $x is always interpreted as Literal characters, **not** as a shell variable.

The -f option avoids issues related to command line quoting. But it introduces some complexity, because now you have a separate file to maintain.

Chapter 19

Using sed within Shell Scripts

sed is often best used from within a shell script, as a one-line command. Here is a shell script segment, with a one-line sed command included:

```
if [ ! -s $f_1 ]; then break; fi
if [ ! -s $f_2 ]; then break; fi
sed "s/ */ /g" $f_1 > $patfile
grep -f $patfile $f_2 > $outfile
```

For a more complex sed script, you can, as in the following shell script segment: 1) First, build an external sed script file (called 'sf' here); 2) Then, run the commands in sf (-f sf):

```
echo 's/3[ 0][ 0]/1/' > sf
echo 's/1[ 0][ 0]/3/' >> sf
sed -f sf $infile > $outfile
```

This can simplify troubleshooting, since the lines in sf are not affected by interpretation by the shell, and can be easily viewed. For example, $X in sf always means the Literal characters '$X', and not the shell variable.

This can also make the sed syntax cleaner and easier to read, instead of trying to jam the entire script all on one command line. And you get the benefit of a separate file created dynamically when you need it.

Finally, you can put a sed script in an executable file with a special '#!' first line ('shebang' line):

```
$ cat shebang.sed
#!/bin/sed -f
s/red/xxx/
s/BLUE/1234/
```

You can directly run shebang.sed, assuming the file permissions are set correctly:

General Advice about sed

```
$ shebang.sed rgb
lower (#1): "xxx green blue"
UPPER (#2): "RED GREEN 1234"
```

This is equivalent to running:

```
$ sed -f shebang.sed rgb
lower (#1): "xxx green blue"
UPPER (#2): "RED GREEN 1234"
```

Testing sed Scripts

It is often a good idea to do some experiments on test data, before running a sed script (or any kind of program) on the actual data. Or run the sed script on the actual data, but use Unix 'diff' to verify that the changes were as you expected.

A stream editor saves you many hours, compared with hand editing. It is worth taking a few extra minutes, to make sure your script is making the changes you intended. You must insure correct operation before making any permanent changes to your data files.

Testing a sed script is not that much different from testing any script or program, no what what language you use. It's often a good idea to get something simple working first. Then, think of every kind of input data that "might happen", and construct test cases to make sure the script handles them correctly.

Structuring Input Files

You can save yourself much time and effort by properly structuring input source code and other text files. The benefits will apply regardless of how you process your files (with sed or with any of numerous other ways).

Chapter 19

An example of a good (logically organized) way to structure text:

> This chapter introduces Unix OS.
> Unix OS was developed in 1969
> (at Bell Labs, in New Jersey),
> and soon caught on.

An example of a poor (random and haphazard) way to structure text:

> This chapter introduces Unix
> OS. Unix OS was developed in
> 1969 (at Bell Labs, in New
> Jersey), and soon caught on.

You can use sed to build complex scripts to find (and change) phrases that span lines, such as 'Unix OS' and 'New Jersey' in example #2 above.

But an ounce of prevention is worth a pound of cure. Instead of wasting time with complex (and error-prone) efforts to match phrases that span lines, simply keep phrases (like 'New Jersey') on one line.

Here are some additional ways to keep text files, such as books and user guides, from getting all jumbled:

- Put each sentence on a separate line.
- Maybe split a sentence after a comma.
- Maybe split a sentence at parentheses.
- Put a blank line between paragraphs.

There are many common-sense ways to make your files easier to maintain. For example, there is no point mixing <HR> and <hr> HTML tags. Always use either upper or (preferred) lower case.

Again, there is no point mixing <b> and <strong> tags. They both produce bold text. So always use <b> or (preferred) <strong>.

If you inherit poorly structured text, it is usually a good idea to clean up the file (impose structure) as a first step. In the long run, you will save time and prevent mistakes. sed can help automate any initial cleanup.

If you edit source code files, maintaining good structure is very important. Besides making the files easier to edit with sed, good formatting makes the code much easier to read.

In most languages, even very sloppily formatted code will compile and run correctly. But maintenance and readability are compromised.

Good code layout relates to white space, blank lines, indentation, block structure format, and other consistent coding standards. The goal is to show the logical

General Advice about sed

structure of the program, for better readability and maintainability.

More explanation concerning source code layout is far beyond the scope of this book. "Code Complete", by Steve McConnell, discusses source code layout and style in detail, and is recommended.

If you edit data files, the structure is probably out of your control. Luckily, most data files have a very regular structure, because they would not otherwise function for their purpose. Here are typical examples:

```
00000300101444000101
00000400101444000101
00000500101544146000
```

```
001 0 179 172 68 64 88 85 4 4
001 1 184 175 68 65 89 84 4 3
001 2 187 177 68 67 86 82 4 4
```

In summary, aim for clean, structured input files, and simpler sed commands. Avoid disorganized, unstructured input files, and more complex sed commands.

And keep in mind that any powerful tool, including sed, can be a double-edged sword. It pays to double-check, to do some small experiments, before making widespread, global changes.

Making full daily (or more frequent) backups of your files is a good idea. That way, if error occurs, either from sed or in any of countless other ways, you can go back to a valid copy.

Also, you can use the Unix diff command, automated from with a shell script, to examine and verify the differences between an input file and the edited version:

```
$ sed 's/RED/123/' rgb > a.txt
$ diff rgb a.txt
2c2
< UPPER (#2): "RED GREEN BLUE"
---
> UPPER (#2): "123 GREEN BLUE"
```

At this point, you have covered every feature of sed. The next chapters (20-26) show and explain many examples of sed scripts, to give you more practice.

20: Examples - Substitution

The s command, for doing substitutions, is the most commonly used sed command. There are countless ways to do substitutions (using the regular expressions explained in Chapters 1-9). This chapter shows a few typical examples.

Do a Simple Substitution

To change all instances of 'r3d2' to 'r2d2':

```
$ echo r3d2 | sed 's/r3d2/r2d2/g'
r2d2
```

Substitute for a Span

To substitute 'X' for a span of two consecutive digits:

```
$ seq 8 11 | sed "s/[0-9]\{2\}/X/"
8
9
X
X
```

The character set '[0-9]' represents a single digit, and '\{2\}' means 'two of the previous character, character set, or group'. The replacement is 'X'.

Add Leader at Line Start

To add some periods at the beginning of each line:

```
$ sed "s/^/.../" rgb
...lower (#1): "red green blue"
...UPPER (#2): "RED GREEN BLUE"
```

The special '^' character means 'start of PatSpace'.

Delete Space at Line Start

To remove spaces, but only from the beginning of each line:

```
$ echo "   xx" | sed "s/^ *//"
xx
```

' *' means zero or more spaces. The '^' anchors the pattern to the start of PatSpace.

Delete Space at Line End

To remove spaces, but only from the end of each line:

```
$ echo "xx   " | sed "s/ *$//"
xx
```

The special '$' character means 'end of PatSpace'. So zero or more (*) spaces at the end of the line are removed.

Chapter 20

Substitute only for a Word

To replace the word 'am' with '99':

```
$ echo am | sed "s/\<am\>/99/g"
99
$ echo amp | sed "s/\<am\>/99/g"
amp
```

sed defines a 'Word' as a sequence of letters, numbers, and the '_' character. So 'am-4' is two words, separated by a hyphen.

Substitute for One or More (+)

To substitute a single 'g' for one or more 'g' characters:

```
$ echo longggg | sed "s/g\+/g/"
long
```

Substitute up to Something

This example is worthy of close study, because it is often useful, and is perhaps a little difficult to understand at first. To substitute for a span up to a certain character (':' in this case):

```
$ echo a:b:c | sed "s/[^:]\+:/x:/"
x:b:c
```

The search pattern is the longest sequence of characters that are 'not colon', followed by a single ':' character. If the search pattern is found, it is replaced with the 'x:' sequence.

Substitute on Certain Lines

To substitute only on certain lines (those with the letter 'x' in this case):

```
$ echo x:3 | sed "/x/ s/3/99/g"
x:99
$ echo y:3 | sed "/x/ s/3/99/g"
y:3
```

In this example, because the /x/ Address is used, the s command only runs if PatSpace contains 'x' (the first case).

Replace with Entire Match

To use the entire matching sequence in the replacement pattern:

```
$ echo one:two | sed "s/on./(&)/"
(one):two
```

The matching sequence is 'on' followed by one character. The '&' inserts the matching sequence, and it is surrounded by parentheses.

Replace All or Just One

To replace the pattern 'aa' with '99' every time the pattern is found (g flag), or only the second time the pattern is found (n flag, with value of 2):

```
$ echo aa:aa | sed "s/aa/99/g"
99:99
$ echo aa:aa | sed "s/aa/99/2"
aa:99
```

21: Examples - Line Spacing

Examples in this chapter:

- Double Space a Stream
- Triple Space a Stream
- Squeeze Blank Lines to One

Double Space a Stream

Two methods are shown:

- G command.
- s command.

```
$ seq 2 | sed 'G'
1

2

```

- G appends HoldSpace to PatSpace.
- PatSpace (1\n and 2\n) AutoPrints.

Examples - Line Spacing

```
$ seq 2 | sed 's/.*/&\n/'
1

2

```

- s replaces '.*' with '&\n'.
- PatSpace ('1\n' and '2\n') AutoPrints.

Triple Space a Stream

Again, two methods are shown (results not displayed).

```
$ seq 2 | sed 'G; G'
```

- G appends HoldSpace to PatSpace twice.
- PatSpace (1\n\n and 2\n\n) AutoPrints.

```
$ seq 2 | sed 's/.*/&\n\n/'
```

- s replaces '.*' with '&\n\n'.
- PatSpace (1\n\n and 2\n\n) AutoPrints.

Chapter 21

Squeeze Blank Lines to One

```
$ cat sq.sed
/^$/ N; /\n$/ D
```

This sed script (equivalent to 'cat -s') changes a series of blank lines to one blank line. The script 1) reads next line if PatSpace is blank, then 2) deletes line #1 of PatSpace if last line read was blank.

There are four scenarios, to study how it works:

1) Non-blank line (such as 'X'):

```
$ echo X | sed -f sq.sed
X
```

- ^$ does not match PatSpace. N not run.
- \n$ does not match PatSpace. D not run.
- 'X' AutoPrints. Restart Cycle.

2) Blank line, followed by 'X' line:

```
$ cat sq.sed
/^$/ N; /\n$/ D
```

```
$ echo -e "\nX" | sed -f sq.sed

X
```

- ^$ matches. N appends \nX to PatSpace.
- \n$ does not match PatSpace. D not run.
- PatSpace (\nX) AutoPrints.

3) Two blank lines, then 'X' line:

```
$ echo -e "\n\nX" | sed -f sq.sed

X
```

- ^$ matches PatSpace. N appends '\n'.
- D deletes PatSpace line #1.
- Restart script (no line read).

- ♦ ^$ matches PatSpace. N appends '\nX'.
- ♦ \n$ does not match. D is not run.
- ♦ PatSpace (\nX) AutoPrints.

---

4) Two blank lines, at end of stream:

```
$ cat sq.sed
/^$/ N; /\n$/ D
```

```
$ echo -e "\n" | sed -f sq.sed

```

- ^$ matches PatSpace. N appends \n.
- D deletes PatSpace line #1.
- Restart script (no line read).

- ^$ matches PatSpace.
- No more input, so N exits.
- AutoPrint PatSpace (' '). Exit sed.

22: Examples - Add Some Lines

Examples in this chapter:

- Add Line Before Lines 1, 3, ...
- Add Line After Lines 2, 3, ...

- Add Line Before Matching Line
- Add Line After Matching Line
- Add Line Before & After Line

Add Line Before Lines 1, 3, ...

```
$ seq 3 | sed '1~2i xxx'
xxx
1
2
xxx
3
```

- '1~2' Address means First=1, Step=2.
- So 'i' inserts 'xxx' before lines 1, 3, etc.

Add Line After Lines 2, 3, ...

```
$ seq 3 | sed '2~1a xxx'
1
2
xxx
3
xxx
```

Examples - Add Some Lines

- '2~1' Address means First=2, Step=1.
- So 'a' appends 'xxx' after lines 2, 3, etc.

Add Line Before Matching Line

We can either use the p command (print a blank line) or s command (add a blank line into PatSpace).

```
$ seq 2 | sed '/2/ {x; p; x}'
1

2
```

- Line #1 AutoPrints unchanged.
- Line #2 matches, so '{x; p; x}' runs.

♦ x swaps PatSpace (2) and HoldSpace (' ').
♦ p prints PatSpace (' ') (blank line).
♦ x swaps PatSpace (' ') and HoldSpace (2).
♦ PatSpace (2) AutoPrints.

```
$ seq 2 | sed '/2/ s/.*/\n&/'
1

2
```

- Line #1 AutoPrints unchanged.
- Line #2 matches, so s command runs.

♦ s replaces '.*' (PatSpace) with '\n&'.
♦ '\n2' (PatSpace) AutoPrints.

Chapter 22

Add Line After Matching Line

We can either use the G command or s command to append a newline to PatSpace.

```
$ seq 2 | sed '/1/ G'
1

2
```

- Line #1 matches. G is run.
- G appends \n (newline) to PatSpace.
- PatSpace (1\n) AutoPrints.
- Line #2 AutoPrints unchanged.

```
$ seq 2 | sed '/1/ s/.*/&\n/'
1

2
```

- Line #1 matches. s command is run.
- s replaces '.*' with '&\n'.
- PatSpace (1\n) AutoPrints.
- Line #2 AutoPrints unchanged.

Add Line Before & After Line

```
$ seq 2 | sed '/1/{x; p; x; G}'

1

2
```

This combines the two preceding examples. For lines matching RegEx ('1' in this case):

- 'x; p; x;' adds a blank line before.
- G adds a blank line after.

```
$ seq 2 | sed '/1/ s/.*/\n&\n/'

1

2
```

This also combines two of the preceding examples. For lines matching RegEx (again '1'):

- '.*' matches the entire PatSpace.
- s replaces .* with '\n&\n'.
- This adds blank lines before and after.

23: Examples - Print Some Lines

Examples in this chapter:

- Print Line #X
- Print Last Line
- Print Lines L to H
- Print First X Lines
- Print Last X Lines
- Print Lines 4, 8, ...
- Print Matching Line
- Print Line Before Match
- Print Line After Match
- Number Lines in Stream

Print Line #X

```
$ seq 9 | sed -n '5 p'
5
```

- -n option turns off AutoPrint.
- p prints PatSpace on line #5 (X = 5).

Print Last Line

```
$ seq 9 | sed -n '$ p'
9
```

- sed command uses -n option.
- So lines 1-8 do not AutoPrint.
- '$ p' prints last line (9).

```
$ seq 9 | sed '$! d'
9
```

- $! means 'not last line'.
- So '$! d' deletes lines 1-8.
- Last line (9) AutoPrints.

Print Lines L to H

```
$ seq 9 | sed -n '4,5 p'
4
5
```

For this example, L = 4, H = 5:

- -n option turns off AutoPrint.
- p prints PatSpace on lines 4-5.

Print First X Lines

```
$ seq 9 | sed '3 q'
1
2
3
```

- sed AutoPrints Lines 1-2.
- '3q' is run on line #3 (X = 3).
- q AutoPrints PatSpace, exits.

Chapter 23

Print Last X Lines

```
$ seq 5 | sed ':k $q; N; 4,$D; bk'
3
4
5
```

For this example, X = 3:

- Input line #1 read into PatSpace ('1').
- :k Label is ignored. $q is skipped.
- N appends line #2 to PatSpace (1\n2).
- 4,$D is skipped. bk branches to :k.

- ♦ $q does not run (not last line).
- ♦ N appends line #3 to PatSpace (1\n2\n3).
- ♦ 4,$D is skipped. bk branches to :k.

- $q does not run (not last line).
- N appends line #4 (1\n2\n3\n4).
- 4,$D deletes PatSpace line #1 (2\n3\n4).
- bk branches to :k Label.

- ♦ $q does not run (not last line).
- ♦ N appends line #5 (2\n3\n4\n5).
- ♦ 4,$D deletes PatSpace line #1 (3\n4\n5).
- ♦ bk branches to :k Label.

- $q exits script (last line).
- PatSpace AutoPrints (3\n4\n5).

```
$ seq 5 | sed ':k $q; N; 4,$D; bk'
3
4
5
```

The previous example is useful for learning sed and works perfectly. But in practice, one would of course use 'tail -n 3' (Chapter 28) to print the last 3 lines.

Print Lines 4, 8, ...

```
$ seq 9 | sed -n '4~4 p'
4
8
```

- -n option turns off AutoPrint.
- '4~4' Address means First=4, Step=4.
- So p runs every 4th line: 4, 8, etc.

Print Matching Line

```
$ seq 9 | sed -n '/5/ p'
5
```

- sed command uses -n option.
- So non-matching lines do not AutoPrint.
- '/5/ p' prints matching line (5).

Print Line Before Match

For purposes of display in this ebook, the script is a little long for the command line. So we use the -f option and put the script in a separate file.

```
$ cat pl-bm.sed
/5/ {x; 1!p; x}; h
```

```
$ seq 9 | sed -n -f pl-bm.sed
4
```

Chapter 23

- sed command uses -n option.
- So PatSpace does not AutoPrint.

♦ Line #5 matches '5'. So { } and h run.
♦ Other lines just run h (hold PatSpace).

- x swaps HoldSpace and PatSpace.
- That puts the prior line into PatSpace.
- If not line #1 (1!), p prints PatSpace.
- x swaps PatSpace and HoldSpace.

The following example verifies that the script prints the line before the match, in the case of multiple matches in adjacent lines:

```
$ cat pl-bm.sed
/5/ {x; 1!p; x}; h
$ seq 49 52 | sed -n -f pl-bm.sed
49
50
51
```

Print Line After Match

```
$ cat pl-am.sed
/5/ {:k n; p; /5/ bk}
```

```
$ seq 9 | sed -n -f pl-am.sed
6
```

- If not line #5, { } does not run.
- No lines AutoPrint, because of -n.
- Line #5 matches '/5/'. So { } runs:

♦ n reads next line ('6') into PatSpace.

Examples - Print Some Lines

- ◆ -n option stops AutoPrint by n command.
- ◆ p prints PatSpace ('6').

- PatSpace ('6') does not match '/5/'.
- So b does not branch.

What if there are multiple matches, in adjacent lines? In that case, b branches, n reads the next line, and p prints it.

```
$ cat pl-am.sed
/5/ {:k n; p; /5/ bk}
$ seq 49 52 | sed -n -f pl-am.sed
51
52
```

Number Lines in Stream

```
$ seq 2 | sed = | sed 'N; s!\n! !'
1 1
2 2
```

sed command #1 ('sed =') prints the line number on a separate line. The result is 4 lines: 1, 1, 2, 2.

sed command #2 joins lines together. N appends the next line to PatSpace, after \n (newline). s changes the newline to a space.

```
$ seq 2 | sed = | sed 'N; s!\n!\t!'
```

Alternatively, in above example (results not shown), sed changes \n to \t (tab).

Because numbering lines is so useful, there is also a special Unix utility ('nl') totally dedicated to just that task.

24: Examples - Delete Some Lines

Examples in this chapter:

- Delete Line #X
- Delete Last Line
- Delete Lines L to H

- Delete First X Lines
- Delete Last X Lines
- Delete Lines 1, 3, ...

- Delete All Blank Lines
- Delete Leading Blank Lines
- Delete Up to Blank Line #1

- Delete Match-Based Range
- Delete Following Matched Line
- Delete Serial Duplicate Lines

Delete Line #X

```
$ seq 3 | sed '2d'
1
3
```

For this example, X = 2:

- Only line #2 runs d command.
- d deletes PatSpace, starts new Cycle.
- Other lines AutoPrint PatSpace.

Delete Last Line

```
$ seq 3 | sed '$ d'
1
2
```

- Only line #3 ($) runs d command.
- d deletes PatSpace, starts new Cycle.
- Other lines AutoPrint PatSpace.

Delete Lines L to H

```
$ seq 9 | sed '2,8 d'
1
9
```

For this example, L = 2, H = 8:

- Lines 2-8 run the d command.
- d deletes PatSpace, starts new Cycle.
- Other lines AutoPrint PatSpace.

Delete First X Lines

```
$ seq 6 | sed '1,4d'
5
6
```

For this example, X = 4:

- Lines 1-4 are in 1,4 range. So d runs.
- Lines 5-6 not in range. So d not run.

Chapter 24

Delete Last X Lines

```
$ cat dl-nl.sed
:k $d; N; 2,7 bk
P; D
```

```
$ seq 9 | sed -f dl-nl.sed
1
2
```

For this example, X = 7 ('2,7'):

- b last branches on line #7:
- PatSpace = '1\n2\n3\n4\n5\n6\n7'

♦ N appends '8' to PatSpace, after \n.
♦ P prints '1'. D deletes '1\n' in PatSpace.
♦ N appends '9' to PatSpace, after \n.
♦ P prints '2'. D deletes '2\n' in PatSpace.
♦ $d deletes PatSpace. No more input.

If only 1-7 lines in input stream:

- $d runs before P prints any output.
- So no output (the desired result).

This example is useful for learning sed and works perfectly. But in practice, one would of course use 'head -n -7' (Chapter 28) to delete the last 7 lines.

Delete Lines 1, 3, ...

```
$ seq 5 | sed '1~2 d'
2
4
```

- '1~2' Address means First=1, Step=2.
- So d runs on odd-numbered lines.

- sed reads each line into PatSpace.
- Lines 1, 3, 5 (odd) are deleted.
- Lines 2, 4 (even) are not deleted.

Delete All Blank Lines

```
$ echo -e "\nA"

A
$ echo -e " \nA"

 A
```

Two sample inputs are shown above:

- Blank line from '\nA' is totally empty.
- Blank line from ' \nA' has one space.

```
$ echo -e "\nA" | sed '/^$/d'
A
$ echo -e " \nA" | sed '/^$/d'

 A
```

- '/^$/' only matches empty PatSpace.
- So blank line with spaces is not deleted.

```
$ echo -e "\nA" | sed '/^ *$/d'
A
$ echo -e " \nA" | sed '/^ *$/d'
A
```

- '/^ *$/' matches 0 or more spaces.
- So either blank line is deleted.

Chapter 24

Delete Leading Blank Lines

```
$ echo -e "\nA\n"

A

```

```
$ echo -e "\nA\n" | sed '/./,$! d'
A

```

'/./,$' means 'first non-blank line (line with A) to last line'. The opposite expression '/./,$!' means 'blank lines at top of file'.

Delete Up to Blank Line #1

```
$ echo -e "H\n\nB"
H

B
```

```
$ echo -e "H\n\nB" | sed '1,/^$/ d'
B
```

'1,/^$/' means 'from line #1 to first blank line'. This is useful for deleting a header from a file. Imagine that 'H' is the multi-line header section, and 'B' is the multi-line body section.

Delete Match-Based Range

```
$ seq 6 | sed '/2/,/5/ d'
1
6
```

- Lines 2-5 are in '/2/,/5/' range. d runs.
- 1 and 6 not in range. So d not run.

Delete Following Matched Line

```
$ seq 3 | sed '/1/ {n; /2/ d}'
1
3
```

- Line #1 PatSpace matches '/1/' Address.
- So { } group runs on line #1.
- n prints PatSpace, reads next line.
- PatSpace ('2') matches '/2/' Address.
- d deletes PatSpace, restarts script.

———

```
$ seq 3 | sed '/1/ { n; /3/ d }'
1
2
3
```

- Line #1 PatSpace matches '/1/' Address.
- So { } group runs on line #1.
- n prints PatSpace, reads next line.
- PatSpace does **not** match '/3/' Address.
- d is **not** run. AutoPrint PatSpace line #3.

———

The point is that you could use more complex regular expressions than '/1/' and '/2/' to selectively delete a matching line, when it directly follows another matching line.

Chapter 24

Delete Serial Duplicate Lines

```
$ cat sdl.txt
X
X
Y
Z
Z
```

```
$ cat dsdl.sed
$!   N; /^\(.*\)\n\1$/!   P; D
```

```
$ sed -f dsdl.sed sdl.txt
X
Y
Z
```

The '`^\(.*\)\n\1$`' RegEx:

- Starts with '\(.*\)' (save to \1).
- Has '\n' (newline) in the middle.
- Ends with \1 (play back saved).

So '/^\(.*\)\n\1$/!   P' only runs P if adjacent lines are **not** the same. That is the key to squeezing down duplicate lines.

N and D form a pair:

- N reads the next line.
- D deletes the previously read line.

♦ 'X' read into PatSpace. Not last line.
♦ So N appends '\nX' to PatSpace ('X').
♦ 'X\nX' matches '^\(.*\)\n\1$', so skip P.
♦ D restarts script, with 'X' PatSpace.

- N appends '\nY' to PatSpace ('X').
- 'X\nY' does not match '^\(.*\)\n\1$'.
- So P prints PatSpace line #1 ('X').
- D restarts script, with 'Y' PatSpace.

Examples - Delete Some Lines

- ♦ N appends '\nZ' to PatSpace ('Y').
- ♦ 'Y\nZ' does not match '^\(.*\)\n\1$'.
- ♦ So P prints PatSpace line #1 ('Y').
- ♦ D restarts script, with 'Z' PatSpace.

- N appends '\nZ' to PatSpace ('Z').
- 'Z\nZ' matches '^\(.*\)\n\1$', so skip P.
- D restarts script, with 'Z' PatSpace.

- ♦ Is last line, so N does not run.
- ♦ 'Z' does not match '^\(.*\)\n\1$'.
- ♦ So P prints PatSpace line #1 ('Z').
- ♦ D deletes PatSpace. No more input.

```
$ cat dsdl.sed
$!   N;  /^\(.*\)\n\1$/!   P; D
```

This example is useful for learning sed and works perfectly. But in practice, one would of course use 'uniq' (Chapter 28) to delete extra adjacent duplicate lines.

25: Examples - Other Short Tasks

Examples in this chapter do various tasks:

- Count Lines in Stream
- Delete Duplicate Characters
- Format a Phone Number
- Capitalize Words
- Replace First Match in File

- Reverse Each Word
- Reverse Each Line
- Reverse Order of Lines
- Add Commas to Numbers

Count Lines in Stream

```
$ sed -n '$ =' a-i.txt
9
```

- = command is run if last line ($).
- = prints the line number (9).
- -n option stops default output.

Of course, "wc -l a-i.txt" is a simpler and better way to count lines.

Delete Duplicate Characters

```
$ echo aab|sed -r 's/(.)\1+/\1/g'
ab
```

The script replaces consecutive repeated characters. For example, the script would change 'c=aaa=bb=c=d' to 'c=a=b=c=d'.

- '(.)\1+' matches consecutive duplicates.
- '(.)' saves the duplicated character.
- \1 SubEx replaces duplicates with just one.

Format a Phone Number

```
$ cat p.sed
s/[0-9]{3}/(&) /
s/([0-9]{3})([0-9]{4})/\1-\2/
```

```
$ echo 1112223333 | sed -rf p.sed
(111) 222-3333
```

- s command #1 formats area code.
- s command #2 formats rest of number.

Capitalize Words

```
$ sed 's:\w\+:\u&:g' rgb
Lower (#1): "Red Green Blue"
UPPER (#2): "RED GREEN BLUE"
```

- '\w\+' matches a Word (one or more \w).
- '\u&' makes the first letter uppercase.

Chapter 25

Replace First Match in File

```
$ cat rfm-if.sed
/#/ {s//=/; :k n; bk}
```

```
$ sed -f rfm-if.sed rgb
lower (=1): "red green blue"
UPPER (#2): "RED GREEN BLUE"
```

- 's//=/' replaces previous RegEx specified.
- ':k n; bk' repeatedly runs n command.
- This prints remaining lines in stream.

- ◆ First time '#' matches, { } runs.
- ◆ s replaces '#' with '=';
- ◆ Loop prints remaining lines, as is.

Reverse Each Word

```
$ cat rew.sed
s/\w+/\n&/g
:k s/(\w*\n)(\w)/\2\1/g; tk
s/\n//g
```

```
$ sed -rf rew.sed rgb
rewol (#1): "der neerg eulb"
REPPU (#2): "DER NEERG EULB"
```

The rew.sed script has three parts. Each part is on a separate script line:

- \n separator put before each Word.
- The loop reverses each Word.
- The \n separators are all deleted.

Examples - Other Short Tasks

In step #2 (the loop), s is run repeatedly. Each time s runs, it swaps the positions of:

- '\w*\n' (\n and any Word before)
- '\w' (Word character after \n)

How the Word 123 is reversed to 321:
\n123   1\n23   21\n3   321\n

t finally fails to branch when s does not run (because no Word character after \n). At that point, the final s runs to delete \n separators, and PatSpace is printed.

Reverse Each Line

```
$ cat rel.sed
s/$/\n/
:k s/(.)(\n.*)/\2\1/; tk
s/^\n//
```

```
$ echo ABCDEF | sed -rf rel.sed
FEDCBA
$ echo 123 | sed -rf rel.sed
321
```

The rel.sed script has three parts. Each part is on a separate script line:

- \n separator is appended to the line.
- The loop reverses the line.
- The \n separator is deleted.

In step #2 (the loop), s is run repeatedly. Each time s runs, it swaps the positions of:

- '\n.*' (\n and everything after)
- '.' (the character in front of \n)

How the line 123 is reversed to 321:
123\n   12\n3   1\n32   \n321

t finally fails to branch when s does not run (because no character in front of \n).

163

Chapter 25

Reverse Order of Lines

```
$ seq 3 | sed '1!G; h; $!d'
3
2
1
```

- 1! means 'is not first line'.
- $! means 'is not last line'.

- Line #1 is read into PatSpace.
- 1!G is skipped, because line #1.
- h copies PatSpace ('1') to HoldSpace.
- $!d deletes PatSpace, starts new Cycle.

- Line #2 is read into PatSpace.
- 1!G appends HoldSpace to PatSpace.
- h copies PatSpace (2\n1) to HoldSpace.
- $!d deletes PatSpace, starts new Cycle.

- Line #3 is read into PatSpace.
- 1!G appends HoldSpace to PatSpace.
- h copies PatSpace (3\n2\n1) to HoldSpace.
- Skip $!d (last line). AutoPrint PatSpace.

Here is an alternate way to reverse the order of lines. '$!d' has the same effect as using $p with the -n option:

```
$ seq 3 | sed -n '1!G; h; $p'
3
2
1
```

Of course, 'tac' (Chapter 29) is so much simpler for reversing line order in a file. But at least the examples show how G and h can cooperate to accumulate lines.

Add Commas to Numbers

```
$ cat cm.sed
:k
s/(.*[0-9])([0-9]{3})/\1,\2/
tk
```

```
$ echo 1234567 | sed -rf cm.sed
1,234,567
```

- -r option makes syntax easier to read.
- s looks for the RegEx: '.*[0-9][0-9]{3}'
- '.*[0-9]' part is saved to \1 BackRef.
- '[0-9]{3}' part is saved to \2 BackRef.
- Greedy '.*' forces '[0-9]{3}' to the right.

If the RegEx is found, s inserts a comma and t branches. If the RegEx is **not** found, s does not replace, t does not branch, script ends, and AutoPrint PatSpace.

Loop #1 - The RegEx matches 1234567; s changes 1234567 to 1234,567; t branches.
Loop #2 - The RegEx matches 1234; s changes 1234 to 1,234; t branches.
Loop #3 - The RegEx is not found; s does not replace; t does not branch; the script ends; PatSpace (1,234,567) AutoPrints.

26: Examples - Complex Tasks

This chapter has a few examples of longer, more complex sed scripts. The chapter also shows how sed fits within shell scripts. Examples in this chapter do various tasks:

- Add Headers and Footers
- Multi-Line Find and Replace
- Set Incremental Macro Values
- Delete HTML Tags

Add Headers and Footers

The example in this section adds a header and footer to each paragraph. Here is the sed script:

```
$ cat add-hf.sed
/./ {H; $!  d}; x; /^$/ b
s/^/HDR/; s/$/\nFTR/
$!   s/$/\n/
```

Paragraphs are separated with an empty line (^$). The add-hf.sed script adds a HDR line before each paragraph, and a FTR line after each paragraph. Suppose the input file has one paragraph:

```
Paragraph Line 1
Paragraph Line 2
```

Examples - Complex Tasks

Here is the result (sed output) of running the script on the paragraph:

```
HDR
Paragraph Line 1
Paragraph Line 2
FTR
```

The add-hf.sed script has three parts. Each part is on a separate script line:

1) Gather up and position paragraph lines.
2) Add HDR and FTR around the paragraph.
3) Add \n separator if not last paragraph.

```
$ cat add-hf.sed
/./ {H; $! d}; x; /^$/ b
s/^/HDR/; s/$/\nFTR/
$!   s/$/\n/
```

'/./ {H; $! d}' uses H to append (gather up) paragraph lines to HoldSpace. d effectively gets the next input line.

x swaps the paragraph back into PatSpace at the appropriate time, either at a blank line after a paragraph ({ } did not run), or at the last line of the last paragraph (d did not run).

'/^$/ b' branches to end of script, where a blank line AutoPrints, at the appropriate time: Blank line at top of file, or second of two blank lines between paragraphs.

'$! s/$/\n/' adds the separator between paragraphs, and does not run after last paragraph in the file.

Chapter 26

Scenario #1 to test is 'paragraph is **not** last in the file':

- Each paragraph line runs '/./ { }' group.
- H appends text to HoldSpace.
- d deletes PatSpace, reads next input line.

At empty line after paragraph:

- { } is not run. x swaps. b does not branch.
- s inserts HDR; s appends FTR.
- s adds \n (paragraph separator).
- AutoPrint PatSpace.

```
$ cat add-hf.sed
/./ {H; $!  d}; x; /^$/ b
s/^/HDR/; s/$/\nFTR/
$!  s/$/\n/
```

Scenario #2 to test is 'last paragraph in the file, and ends on last line of the file':

- Each paragraph line runs '/./ { }' group.
- H appends text to HoldSpace.
- d deletes PatSpace, reads next input line.

The last line in the paragraph (last line of file) runs differently:

- { } runs, but d not run (last line).
- x swaps. b does not run.
- s adds HDR before, FTR after.
- s does **not** add \n (separator).
- AutoPrint PatSpace.

```
$ cat add-hf.sed
/./ {H; $!  d}; x; /^$/ b
s/^/HDR/; s/$/\nFTR/
$!  s/$/\n/
```

Examples - Complex Tasks

Scenario #3 to test is 'last paragraph in the file, and is followed by an empty line':

- Each paragraph line runs '/./ { }' group.
- H appends text to HoldSpace.
- d deletes PatSpace, reads next input line.

At the empty line following the end of the last paragraph:

- { } not run. x swaps. b not run.
- s adds HDR before, FTR after.
- s does **not** add \n (separator).
- AutoPrint PatSpace.

———

The above example proved difficult to figure out on direct inspection. It took several non-trivial scenarios to verify correct operation.

In practice, I might take a simpler and cleaner 'divide and conquer' approach. Instead of doing everything in one sed script, I might split the task into seven steps, combined into a shell script, as outlined below:

1) 'cat -s' squeezes adjacent blank lines.
2) sed '$ { /^$/ d }' deletes blank last line.
3) sed '1 { /^$/ d }' deletes blank first line.

4) sed '1 i HDR' adds HDR before line #1.
5) sed '$ a FTR' adds FTR after last line.
6) sed '/^$/ i HDR' adds other HDR lines.
7) sed '/^$/ a FTR' adds other FTR lines.

It is longer and slower, but each step is easily understood and verified. Legibility and maintainability trump speed and brevity. The shell script still uses sed a lot. But it breaks down the task into easily managed segments.

Chapter 26

Multi-Line Find and Replace

It is better (see Chapter 19) to structure files so that phrases do not span lines. But, if needed, this section shows how to find and replace multi-line phrases ('Unix OpSys' in this example).

```
$ cat s3.sed
s/Unix OpSys/Unix OS/g; bT
:L N; s/Unix *\n *OpSys/Unix\nOS/
:T /Unix *$/ bL
```

```
$ cat os.txt
This chapter introduces Unix OpSys. Unix
OpSys was developed in 1969 (at Bell
Labs, in New Jersey), and soon caught on.
```

```
$ sed -f s3.sed os.txt
This chapter introduces Unix OS. Unix
OS was developed in 1969 (at Bell
Labs, in New Jersey), and soon caught on.
```

- Input line #1 is read.
- s changes 'Unix OpSys' to 'Unix OS'.
- bT branches to :T Label ('Test').

♦ PatSpace ends with 'Unix'.
♦ So bL branches to :L Label ('Loop').

- N appends input line #2.
- s changes multi-line 'Unix OpSys'.

♦ PatSpace does not end with 'Unix'.
♦ So bL does not branch to :L Label.
♦ PatSpace (2 lines) AutoPrints.

Examples - Complex Tasks

- Input line #3 is read.
- 'Unix OpSys' is not in PatSpace.
- So s does not replace. Branch to :T.

♦ PatSpace does not end with 'Unix'.
♦ So bL does not branch to :L Label.
♦ PatSpace (input line #3) AutoPrints.

```
$ cat s3.sed
s/Unix OpSys/Unix OS/g; bT
:L N; s/Unix *\n *OpSys/Unix\nOS/
:T /Unix *$/ bL
```

In the following 's4.sed' variation (suggested to me), one of the b commands now branches to the end of the script, and the test logic is reversed:

```
$ cat s4.sed
s/Unix OpSys/Unix OS/g
:T /Unix *$/ !  b; N
s/Unix *\n *OpSys/Unix\nOS/; bT
```

```
$ cat os.txt
This chapter introduces Unix OpSys. Unix
OpSys was developed in 1969 (at Bell
Labs, in New Jersey), and soon caught on.
```

```
$ sed -f s4.sed os.txt
This chapter introduces Unix OS. Unix
OS was developed in 1969 (at Bell
Labs, in New Jersey), and soon caught on.
```

- Input line #1 is read.
- s changes 'Unix OpSys' to 'Unix OS'.

Chapter 26

- ◆ PatSpace ends with 'Unix'.
- ◆ So b does **not** branch to end.

- N appends input line #2.
- s changes multi-line 'Unix OpSys'.

- ◆ bT branches to :T Label ('Test').
- ◆ PatSpace does not end with 'Unix'.
- ◆ So b branches to end of script.
- ◆ PatSpace (2 lines) AutoPrints.

- Input line #3 is read.
- 'Unix OpSys' is not in PatSpace.
- So s does not replace.

- ◆ PatSpace does not end with 'Unix'.
- ◆ So b branches to end of script.
- ◆ PatSpace (input line #3) AutoPrints.

```
$ cat s4.sed
s/Unix OpSys/Unix OS/g
:T /Unix *$/ !  b; N
s/Unix *\n *OpSys/Unix\nOS/; bT
```

Finally, the 's5.sed' variation (also suggested to me) adds P and D commands, to ensure that sed keeps at most two lines in memory (PatSpace):

```
$ cat s5.sed
s/Unix OpSys/Unix OS/g
:T /Unix *$/ !  b; N
s/Unix *\n *OpSys/Unix\nOS/; P; D
```

```
$ cat os.txt
This chapter introduces Unix OpSys. Unix
OpSys was developed in 1969 (at Bell
Labs, in New Jersey), and soon caught on.
```

Examples - Complex Tasks

```
$ sed -f s5.sed os.txt
This chapter introduces Unix OS. Unix
OS was developed in 1969 (at Bell
Labs, in New Jersey), and soon caught on.
```

- Input line #1 is read.
- s changes 'Unix OpSys' to 'Unix OS'.

♦ PatSpace ends with 'Unix'.
♦ So b does **not** branch to end.

- N appends input line #2.
- s changes multi-line 'Unix OpSys'.

♦ P prints PatSpace line #1 ('This ...').
♦ D deletes PatSpace line #1.
♦ D restarts sed script.

- 'Unix OpSys' is not in PatSpace.
- So s does not replace.

♦ PatSpace does not end with 'Unix'.
♦ So b branches to end of script.
♦ PatSpace ('OS ...') AutoPrints.

- Input line #3 is read.
- 'Unix OpSys' is not in PatSpace.
- So s does not replace.

♦ PatSpace does not end with 'Unix'.
♦ So b branches to end of script.
♦ PatSpace (input line #3) AutoPrints.

```
$ cat s5.sed
s/Unix OpSys/Unix OS/g
:T /Unix *$/ !  b; N
s/Unix *\n *OpSys/Unix\nOS/; P; D
```

Chapter 26

A defect with s3.sed, s4.sed and s5.sed is that the patterns ('Unix OpSys' and 'Unix OS') are hard-coded into the scripts.

To remedy that, and add flexibility, you could run s5.sed from within a shell script.

The shell script could gather the patterns as arguments, use echo to create a customized sed script, and run the sed script.

It is beyond the scope of this book to go into detail about shell scripting. But the next example gives some idea.

Set Incremental Macro Values

This example incrementally sets C 'macro values' to number the Q&A sections in a book, for example 'Question #1', 'Answer #1'. Warning: This is the longest example in the book.

The CNT macro is repeatedly undefined with '#undef CNT', and then defined as 1, 2, etc. Here is a file, before and after processing:

```
...   Omitted text ...
#define CNT 54
...   Omitted text ...
#define CNT 12
...   Omitted text ...
```

```
...   Omitted text ...
#define CNT 1
...   Omitted text ...
#define CNT 2
...   Omitted text ...
```

Here is a shell script, shown in 3 segments, to do the work. It contains two sed commands. 'XYZ' is used as a special marker. In the production shell script, a unique ID (eg, 'XUPKT') is used.

```
f=$DOC_DIR/sed-book.hpp
cp $f /tmp/book.save
sed -i 's/ CNT ..*/ CNT XYZ/' $f
```

Examples - Complex Tasks

```
n=1
while [ 1 -eq 1 ]; do
  echo $n
  grep --quiet XYZ $f
  if [ $? -ne 0 ]; then break; fi
  sed -i "0,/XYZ/ s//$n/" $f
  let "n++"
done
```

```
diff /tmp/book.save $f > diff.x
echo -n "Press Enter key:   "; read
vi diff.x
```

Why use a shell script? Because using Unix utilities within shell scripts is so much more powerful than using sed (or other tool) in isolation.

The shell is a real programming language, and is a convenient way to organize and coordinate other Unix utilities, including sed.

An aside: The C __COUNTER__ macro would not work in this context, because CNT is used multiple times before incrementing.

Here are the details of what the shell and sed commands do:

```
f=$DOC_DIR/sed-book.hpp
cp $f /tmp/book.save
```

- Set 'f' variable to name of input file.
- Use cp to save a copy of input file.

```
sed -i 's/ CNT ..*/ CNT XYZ/' $f
```

- Change ' CNT 54' to ' CNT XYZ'.
- Change ' CNT 12' to ' CNT XYZ'.
- Change any ' CNT ..*' to ' CNT XYZ'.
- $f (input file) is edited 'in place' (-i).

175

Chapter 26

```
n=1
while [ 1 -eq 1 ]; do
  echo $n
```

- Set $n shell variable (counter) to 1.
- Start endless ('1 -eq 1') while loop.
- Use echo to print $n (1 first time).

```
grep --quiet XYZ $f
if [ $? -ne 0 ]; then break; fi
```

- Use grep to see if an 'XYZ' to convert.
- If XYZ found, $? (grep exit status) is 0.
- If not found ('$? -ne 0'), end while loop.

```
sed -i "0,/XYZ/ s//$n/" $f
```

- Use sed to replace XYZ #1 with 1.
- '/XYZ/' is Address of line to run { }.
- 's//$n/' replaces XYZ with $n value ('1').
- Double quotes makes $n shell variable.

♦ '0,/XYZ/' ensures only XYZ #1 is changed.
♦ Lines without XYZ print unchanged.

sed -i "/XYZ/{s//$n/; :k n; bk}" $f also works (replace first XYZ with $n value; then use loop to print rest of file unchanged). But the '0,/XYZ/' method, suggested by Paolo Bonzini, is simpler and more elegant.

```
  let "n++"
done
```

176

- n++ increments shell variable by 1.
- 'done' marks end of while loop.
- Restart while loop, to convert XYZ #2.

———

```
echo -n "Press Enter key:   "; read
diff /tmp/book.save $f > diff.x
vi diff.x
```

- XYZ not found by grep, so loop ended.
- Prompt user ('echo'). Get response ('read').
- Compare new and saved files ('diff').
- Display comparison to user (vi editor).

———

The shell script above works well. But a weakness is that each while loop iteration reads $f from start to finish. With many CNT instances, and a larger input file, it began to slow down.

Since the shell script was run often, and the input file continued to grow, and as an exercise, I decided to rewrite the while loop as a sed script.

———

Here is the sed command (-r allows cleaner syntax, -i edits 'in place') substituted for the while loop, and the script 'set-cnts.sed' run by the sed command:

```
sed -i -r -f set-cnts.sed $f
```

```
# Set counter to 1
1 {h; s/.*/1/; x}

# Replace XYZ with counter
# Increment counter by one
/XYZ/ {
  G; s/(.*) XYZ\n(.*)/\1 \2/
  x; s/.*/expr & + 1/e; x
  }
```

———

Chapter 26

```
# Set counter to 1
1 {h; s/.*/1/; x}
```

- { } runs once, on line #1 of input file.
- h copies (saves) PatSpace to HoldSpace.
- s puts 1 (counter) into PatSpace.
- x swaps line #1 back into PatSpace.

```
# Replace XYZ with counter
# Increment counter by one
/XYZ/ {
  G; s/(.*) XYZ\n(.*)/\1 \2/
  x; s/.*/expr & + 1/e; x
}
```

- { } runs on line with XYZ marker.
- G gets counter from HoldSpace.
- Counter is appended after \n.
- s #1 replaces XYZ with counter.
- The s also gets rid of the \n.

♦ x #1 swaps counter into PatSpace.
♦ x #1 saves edited line to HoldSpace.
♦ s #2 uses 'expr' to add 1 to counter.

- x #2 swaps edited line into PatSpace.
- x #2 saves counter to HoldSpace.
- AutoPrint PatSpace at end of Cycle.

The while loop, at 190 instances of CNT, and 759,000 byte input file size, took 15.5 seconds to change 51 to 1, 12 to 2, etc.

The 'set-cnts.sed' sed script (instead of while loop) took only 0.32 seconds. The while loop and the sed script seem about equal in complexity.

Delete HTML Tags

The next example removes HTML tags. The example was used for this book, to get a word count minus the HTML tags.

Examples - Complex Tasks

If each HTML tag is on a single line (a good idea), and Literal '<' and '>' are **only** used for HTML tags (required), the task is simple:

```
$ cat tags1.html
<p>Sample <b>bold text</b> and
<small>little text</a> to use.
```

```
$ sed 's/<[^>]*>//g' tags1.html
Sample bold text and
little text to use.
```

'[^>]' matches any character **except** '>', so '<[^>]*>' matches an HTML tag. A simpler attempt fails (overextends the match):

```
$ cat tags1.html
<p>Sample <b>bold text</b> and
<small>little text</a> to use.
```

```
$ sed 's/<.*>//g' tags1.html
 and
 to use.
```

If some HTML tags span multiple lines (for better formatting), you will need to do multi-line operations, to find the end of the HTML tag. Here is a test case:

```
$ cat tags2.html
A <table cellpadding="5"
border="0"><tr><td> B
</td></tr></table> C
```

Chapter 26

Here is the sed script to delete HTML tags, even if a tag may extend over several lines. Note that the script has two { } groups (outer and inner):

```
$ cat deltags.sed
/</ {
:k s/<[^>]*>//g; /</ { N; bk }
}
```

```
$ sed -f deltags.sed tags2.html
A  B
 C
```

- Input line #1 is read into PatSpace.
- PatSpace contains '<', so { } runs.
- PatSpace does not contain '>'.
- So s does **not** replace.

- ♦ PatSpace still contains '<'.
- ♦ So inner '{ N; bk }' runs.
- ♦ N appends Line #2 to PatSpace.
- ♦ b loops back to :k Label.

- PatSpace still contains '<'.
- PatSpace now contains '>'.
- So s deletes first 3 tags.

- ♦ Now, no '<' in PatSpace.
- ♦ So inner { } does not run.
- ♦ PatSpace ('A B') AutoPrints.

- Input line #3 is read into PatSpace.
- PatSpace contains '<', so { } runs.
- s deletes last 3 tags.

- ♦ Now, no '<' in PatSpace.
- ♦ So inner { } does not run.
- ♦ PatSpace (' C') AutoPrints.

Examples - Complex Tasks

Here is another test case to show the sed script works correctly. The extra line with 'cellspacing' gets appended by an extra iteration of the bk loop.

```
$ cat tags3.html
A <table cellpadding="5"
cellspacing="0"
border="0"><tr><td> B
</td></tr></table> C
```

```
$ cat deltags.sed
/</ {
:k s/<[^>]*>//g; /</ { N; bk }
}
```

```
$ sed -f deltags.sed tags3.html
A  B
 C
```

There are other ways to delete HTML tags. 'lynx -dump' and the dedicated utility html2text do the same job as the sed script. Once a sed script becomes more complex, it is usually better to switch to a dedicated utility (if available). But because this particular sed script is relatively simple, either way, sed or a dedicated utility, is fine.

27: Related Unix Commands - grep

This chapter explains grep, a powerful Unix utility closely related to sed. The first section shows how to use grep. The second section details the GNU grep command line options.

grep Usage

grep searches an input file or stream for lines containing a match to a RegEx, and prints the matching lines. grep is an efficient and flexible way to find matches and print results.

grep is closely related to ed and sed. The name 'grep' comes from the ed syntax 'g/re/p' (global regular expression print).

```
$ grep red rgb
lower (#1): "red green blue"
```

```
$ sed -n /red/p rgb
lower (#1): "red green blue"
```

grep finds and prints the line containing 'red'. sed can do the same, but grep is simpler and faster.

Like sed, grep can find lines that do **not** contain a RegEx:

```
$ grep -v red rgb
UPPER (#2): "RED GREEN BLUE"
```

Related Unix Commands - grep

```
$ sed -n '/red/! p' rgb
UPPER (#2): "RED GREEN BLUE"
```

Like sed, grep allows case-insensitive matching:

```
$ grep -i red rgb
lower (#1): "red green blue"
UPPER (#2): "RED GREEN BLUE"
```

```
$ sed -n '/red/I p' rgb
lower (#1): "red green blue"
UPPER (#2): "RED GREEN BLUE"
```

Conveniently, grep can automatically include the line number along with the matching line.

```
$ grep -n RED rgb
2:UPPER (#2): "RED GREEN BLUE"
```

When grep and sed do basically the same thing (print lines containing a RegEx), grep is usually the better choice, because grep is simpler and faster. grep supports the full range of regular expressions.

grep and sed work well in tandem. You might use grep to get a subset of lines, and then use sed on the smaller subset. You can use grep for what it can handle, sed for extra capabilities.

The next section explains and illustrates the key GNU grep command line options. Most of these options are shared by other grep versions.

183

Chapter 27

grep Command Line Options

For grep command line options, there is usually a short and a long format. For example, -q is a 'short format' and --quiet is a 'long format'.

The short format always starts with one dash, the long format with two dashes. The two formats produce exactly the same effect. Which format you use is a personal preference.

grep -b   --byte-offset

'grep -b' prefixes matching lines with the byte offset, starting with 0. The example shows (on Unix) the matching lines are at offsets 0 and 2:

```
$ seq 3 | grep -b [12]
0:1
2:2
```

Note that if -o (--only-matching) option is also used, then the byte offset is for the matching part, not for the line.

grep -c   --count

'grep -c' prints a count of matching lines in each input file, instead of printing the actual matching lines.

In combination with -v (--invert-match), -c prints a count of the non-matching lines.

For example, how many of the numbers 1 to 100 contain (or do not contain) at least one of the digits 6, 7, 8?

```
$ seq 100 | grep -c [6-8]
51
$ seq 100 | grep -c -v [6-8]
49
```

grep -e PAT   --regexp=PAT

'grep -e' is used to specify multiple search patterns. The line matches if at least one of the patterns matches.

For example, to match lines containing either "red" or "BLUE":

```
$ grep -e "red" -e "BLUE" rgb
lower (#1): "red green blue"
UPPER (#2): "RED GREEN BLUE"
```

The -e option is also needed if the search pattern starts with a hyphen.

```
$ echo "-xxx" | grep -e "-xxx"
-xxx
```

grep -E   --extended-regexp

'grep -E' switches grep to use extended regular expressions, so that ?, +, {, |, (, and) (no BackSlash) are MetaChars. Avoiding the BackSlash makes the RegEx easier to read. The separate command 'egrep' is the same as 'grep -E'.

Without the -E option, grep uses 'basic regular expressions', so 'x\+' means 'one or more x', and 'x+' means literal 'x+':

```
$ echo "xx" | grep "x\+"
xx
```

With the -E option, 'extended regular expressions' are in effect, so 'x+' means 'one or more x', and 'x\+' means literal 'x' followed by literal '+':

```
$ echo "xx" | grep -E "x+"
xx
```

Chapter 27

grep -F   --fixed-strings

'grep -F' ignores any regular expressions in looking for a match. Instead, grep treats the pattern as a fixed string. For example, with -F in effect, '*' is just the literal asterisk, instead of a MetaChar. The separate command 'fgrep' is the same as 'grep -F'.

The first example uses a character set RegEx to look for a single number, so the line ':1:' contains a match:

```
$ echo ':1:' | grep '[0-9]'
:1:
```

The second example, using -F option, looks for a match to the fixed string in the pattern, and does not interpret '[0-9]' as a character set:

```
$ echo ':1:' | grep -F '[0-9]'
$ echo ':[0-9]:' | grep -F '[0-9]'
:[0-9]:
```

grep -f FILE   --file=FILE

'grep -f FILE' gets the patterns to look for from FILE, instead of from the command line. Each line in FILE has one RegEx (one pattern). red is found, xxx is not found:

```
$ cat grep1.txt
red
xxx
```

```
$ grep -f grep1.txt rgb
lower (#1): "red green blue"
```

If more than one RegEx in the file is found, the matching line is still printed just once:

```
$ cat grep2.txt
red
green
```

```
$ grep -f grep1.txt rgb
lower (#1): "red green blue"
```

grep -H   --with-filename

By default, grep prints the file name (prefixed to the matching line) if multiple input files, and does **not** print the file name if one input file. With 'grep -H', grep always prints the file name.

```
$ grep green rgb
lower (#1): "red green blue"
```

```
$ grep -H green rgb
rgb:lower (#1): "red green blue"
```

grep -h   --no-filename

By default, grep prints the file name (prefixed to the matching line) if multiple input files, and does **not** print the file name if one input file. With 'grep -h', grep never prints the file name.

```
$ grep green rgb rgb
rgb:lower (#1): "red green blue"
rgb:lower (#1): "red green blue"
```

Chapter 27

```
$ grep -h green rgb rgb
lower (#1): "red green blue"
lower (#1): "red green blue"
```

grep --help

'grep --help' prints a useful summary of grep's command line options. 'man grep' gives more details.

grep -i --ignore-case

'grep -i' ignores case when determining if a match.

```
$ grep Blue rgb
$ grep -i Blue rgb
lower (#1): "red green blue"
UPPER (#2): "RED GREEN BLUE"
```

grep -l --files-with-matches

'grep -l' (ell) lists the name of each file that contains a matching line, instead of printing the actual matching lines.

```
$ grep -l red rgb
rgb
$ grep -l xxx rgb
```

This can be very powerful in combination with other Unix commands. For example, to edit all '.c' files containing 'bin2_wt_Dbl':

```
$ vi `grep -l bin2_wt_Dbl *.c`
```

grep -L   --files-without-matches

'grep -L' lists the name of each file **not** containing a matching line, instead of printing the actual matching lines.

```
$ grep -L red rgb
$ grep -L XXXXX rgb
rgb
```

grep -m N   --max-count=N

'grep -m N' stops reading the input file or stream after N matching lines.

```
$ grep ':'  rgb
lower (#1): "red green blue"
UPPER (#2): "RED GREEN BLUE"
```

```
$ grep -m 1 ':'  rgb
lower (#1): "red green blue"
```

grep -n   --line-number

'grep -n' prefixes matching lines with the line number, starting with 1. The example below shows that input lines #1 and #4 match:

```
$ seq 6 9 | grep -n [69]
1:6
4:9
```

grep -o   --only-matching

'grep -o' only prints the matching parts of lines, and puts each matching part on a separate line.

```
$ grep GREEN rgb
UPPER (#2): "RED GREEN BLUE"
$ grep -o GREEN rgb
GREEN
```

```
$ grep -o '\w*RE\w*' rgb
RED
GREEN
```

grep -q   --quiet   --silent

'grep -q' turns off writing to standard output. The $? exit status is 0 if a match is found, otherwise not 0.

```
$ echo Red | grep -q Red
$ echo $?
0
```

```
$ echo Red | grep -q Blue
$ echo $?
1
```

grep -r -R --recursive

'grep -r' searches for patterns in all files under a directory, and under subdirectories.

```
grep -r PATTERN /home/mydir/
```

grep -u --unix-byte-offsets

'grep -u' reports byte offsets as if the file were a Unix file (Unix and Mac computers use a single character to mark the end of a line). The -u option might be used on DOS and Windows computers (which use a two-character combination to mark the end of a line), in combination with the -b option.

```
$ seq 3 | grep -b -u [12]
0:1
2:2
```

grep -v --invert-match

'grep -v' inverts the match sense. Instead of printing matching lines, print non-matching lines.

```
$ grep red rgb
lower (#1): "red green blue"
```

```
$ grep -v red rgb
UPPER (#2): "RED GREEN BLUE"
```

grep -w --word-regexp

'grep -w' only prints a matching line if the pattern exactly matches a whole word, equivalent to using '\<' and '\>'.

```
$ grep blu rgb
lower (#1): "red green blue"
$ grep -w blu rgb
$ grep '\<blu\>' rgb
```

grep -x --line-regexp

'grep -x' only prints a matching line if the pattern exactly matches the entire line, equivalent to using ^ and $.

```
$ grep green rgb
lower (#1): "red green blue"
$ grep -x green rgb
$ grep '^green$' rgb
```

grep -A N --after-context=N

'grep -A N' prints N lines of trailing context, **after** printing a matching line.

```
$ seq 9 | grep -A1 6
6
7
```

The example above printed the matching line (6), followed by one line of trailing context (7).

Related Unix Commands - grep

If more than one matching line, each context group is separated by a group separator (--). Below, group #1 is (2 3), group #2 is (6 7).

```
$ seq 9 | grep -A1 [26]
2
3
--
6
7
```

grep -B N   --before-context=N

'grep -B N' prints N lines of leading context, **before** printing a matching line.

```
$ seq 9 | grep -B1 6
5
6
```

The example above printed the matching line (6), preceded by one line of leading context (5).

If more than one matching line, each context group is separated by a group separator (--). Below, group #1 is (1 2), group #2 is (5 6).

```
$ seq 9 | grep -B1 [26]
1
2
--
5
6
```

193

Chapter 27

grep -C N   --context=N

'grep -C N' prints: 1) N lines of leading context, **before** printing a matching line; and 2) N lines of trailing context, **after** printing a matching line.

```
$ seq 9 | grep -C1 6
5
6
7
```

The example above printed the matching line (6), preceded by one line of leading context (5), and followed by one line of trailing context (7).

If more than one matching line, each context group is separated by a group separator (--). Below, group #1 is (1 2 3), group #2 is (5 6 7).

```
$ seq 9 | grep -C1 [26]
1
2
3
--
5
6
7
```

If the -C context groups overlap, the group separator (--) is not used. Below, group #1 (4 5 6) and group #2 (5 6 7) overlap.

```
$ seq 9 | grep -C1 [56]
4
5
6
7
```

28: Other Related Commands - 1/2

The previous chapter covered grep. This chapter covers additional high priority Unix commands related to sed. With similar syntax and philosophy, sed and these commands complement each other well. The options used by the GNU versions of these utilities are documented and explained in this chapter.

```
head    Print First Few Lines
tail    Print Last Few Lines
uniq    Handle Repeated Lines
tr      Translate Characters
```

Why are there so many small utilities similar to sed? Because they are so useful. If they did not exist, someone would invent them.

Each utility fits in well with the modular Unix philosophy. Each takes a subset of what sed does, and expands it into a powerful utility.

head - Print First Part of File

head is specifically designed to print the first part of a file (or stream), and usually preferable to sed for this purpose. 'head file' (no options) prints the first 10 lines.

head -n N   --lines=N

'head -n N' prints the first N lines:

```
$ seq 3 9 | head -n 2
3
4
```

Chapter 28

head -n -N --lines=-N

'head -n -N' prints the first part of a file, **up to** the last N lines:

```
$ seq 5 | head -n -3
1
2
```

head -c N --bytes=N

'head -c N' prints the first N bytes. The byte count includes \n at the end of a Unix line.

```
$ seq 9 | head -c 4
1
2
```

N (-c N or -n N) takes an optional units suffix. For example, '-c 1b' is the same as '-c 512'. b = 512; kB = 1000; K = 1024; MB = 1000*1000; M = 1024*1024; and so on for G, T, P, E, Z, Y.

head -c -N --bytes=-N

'head -c -N' prints the first part of a file, **up to** the last N bytes. The byte count includes \n at the end of a Unix line.

```
$ seq 4 9 | head -c -8
4
5
```

head -q --quiet --silent

'head -q' omits the single-line header giving the file name, for the case of more than one input file:

```
$ head -q -n 1 rgb rgb
lower (#1): "red green blue"
lower (#1): "red green blue"
```

head -v --verbose

'head -v' prints a single-line header giving the file name, even if only a single input file:

```
$ head -v -n 1 rgb
==> rgb <==
lower (#1): "red green blue"
```

---

tail - Print Last Part of File

tail is specifically designed to print the last part of a file (or stream), and usually preferable to sed for this purpose. 'tail file' (no options) prints the last 10 lines.

tail -n N --lines=N

'tail -n N' prints the last N lines:

```
$ seq 9 | tail -n 2
8
9
```

Chapter 28

tail -n +N   --lines=+N

'tail -n +N' prints the last part of a file, starting with line N:

```
$ seq 4 | tail -n +3
3
4
```

tail -c N   --bytes=N

'tail -c N' prints the last N bytes. The byte count includes \n at the end of a Unix line.

```
$ echo 123456789 | tail -c 3
89
```

N (-c N or -n N) takes an optional units suffix. For example, '-c 1b' is the same as '-c 512'. b = 512; kB = 1000; K = 1024; MB = 1000*1000; M = 1024*1024; and so on for G, T, P, E, Z, Y.

tail -c +N   --bytes=+N

'tail -c +N' prints the last part of a file, starting with byte N:

```
$ echo 123456789 | tail -c +3
3456789
```

tail -f   --follow

'tail -f' does not exit. Instead, it continues to print content appended to a file, such as a log file, as the file grows. Ctrl-C ends 'tail -f'.

```
$ tail -f growing_logfile
```

tail -s N   --sleep-interval=N

'tail -f -s N' sleeps N seconds before rechecking if a file has grown. -s is used in combination with -f.

```
$ tail -f -s 5 growing_log
```

tail -q   --quiet   --silent

'tail -q' omits the single-line header giving the file name, for the case of more than one input file:

```
$ tail -q -n 1 rgb rgb
UPPER (#2): "RED GREEN BLUE"
UPPER (#2): "RED GREEN BLUE"
```

tail -v   --verbose

'tail -v' prints a single-line header giving the file name, even if only a single input file:

```
$ tail -v -n 1 rgb
==> rgb <==
UPPER (#2): "RED GREEN BLUE"
```

Chapter 28

uniq - Handle Repeated Lines

uniq is specifically designed to handle adjacent repeated lines in a file or stream, and usually preferable to sed for this purpose. 'uniq file' (no options) prints only the first of several adjacent repeated lines.

uniq -c --count

'uniq -c' precedes each output line with the number of times the line occurred:

```
$ echo -e "A\nA\nB" | uniq -c
      2 A
      1 B
```

You will normally sort a file before running uniq, because uniq only detects **adjacent** repeated lines. With unsorted input, the results are usually not helpful:

```
$ echo -e "A\nB\nA" | uniq -c
      1 A
      1 B
      1 A
```

uniq -d --repeated

uniq -d (the opposite of -u) only prints repeated lines:

```
$ echo -e "A\nB\nB\nB" | uniq -d
B
```

uniq -f N   --skip-fields=N

'uniq -f N' skips N fields before comparing. Fields are separated by blanks and tabs. To skip 3 fields, then compare 5 characters (compare green with GREEN):

```
$ uniq -f 3 -w 5 rgb
lower (#1): "red green blue"
UPPER (#2): "RED GREEN BLUE"
```

```
$ uniq -i -f 3 -w 5 rgb
lower (#1): "red green blue"
```

uniq -i   --ignore-case

'uniq -i' ignores case when looking for repeating lines:

```
$ echo -e "a\nA" | uniq
a
A
```

```
$ echo -e "a\nA" | uniq -i
a
$ echo -e "A\na" | uniq -i
A
```

Chapter 28

uniq -s N   --skip-chars=N

'uniq -s N' skips the first N characters on each line when determining if the line repeated:

```
$ echo -e "AA\nBA" | uniq
AA
BA
$ echo -e "AA\nBA" | uniq -s 1
AA
```

uniq -u   --unique

'uniq -u' (the opposite of -d) only prints non-repeated lines:

```
$ echo -e "A\nB\nB\nB" | uniq -u
A
```

uniq -w N   --check-chars=N

'uniq -w N' only checks N characters on each line when determining if the line repeated:

```
$ echo -e "AAA\nAA\nA" | uniq
AAA
AA
A
```

```
$ echo -e "AAA\nAA\nA" | uniq -w 2
AAA
A
$ echo -e "AAA\nAA\nA" | uniq -w 1
AAA
```

Other Related Commands - 1/2

The -s and -w options can be used together. 'uniq -s 5 -w 3' skips the first 5 characters, and then checks 3 characters, to determine if the line repeated.

---

tr - Translate Characters

tr translates, squeezes or deletes single input characters. tr is similar to the sed y command, but much easier and better.

tr (a pure filter) only takes input from standard input, and writes output to standard output. In other words:

```
                    Works?
tr abc ABC    in.txt   No
tr abc ABC < in.txt   Yes
```

---

tr translates from 'Set_1' (eg, abc) to 'Set_2' (eg, 123). To translate a to 1, b to 2, c to 3:

```
$ echo abcdef | tr abc 123
123def
```

In contrast to the sed y command, tr accepts character ranges, like a-z or 0-9. To translate a to 1, b to 2, c to 3, d to 4:

```
$ echo abcdef | tr a-d 1-4
1234ef
```

To translate b to X, c to Y, d to Z:

```
$ echo abcdef | tr b-d X-Z
aXYZef
```

Chapter 28

tr -d   --delete

'tr -d Set_1' deletes characters in Set_1. To delete a, b, and c (Set_1 = a-c):

```
$ echo abcdef | tr -d a-c
def
```

To delete null characters (Set_1 = "\000"), assuming nulls.txt includes some null characters:

```
$ tr -d "\000" < nulls.txt
```

tr -s   --squeeze-repeats

'tr -s Set_1' squeezes (translates several in a row to one) characters in Set_1. To squeeze multiple 'x' to one 'x':

```
$ echo xxxxyz | tr -s x
xyz
```

To squeeze empty lines (translate multiple '\n' to one '\n'):

```
$ tr -s '\n' < empty-lns.txt
```

Other Related Commands - 1/2

tr uses Posix character classes, such as [:alpha:], [:blank:], etc. To translate alphabetical characters to '=':

```
$ echo abc123 | tr [:alpha:]  X
XXX123
$ echo abc123 | tr a-zA-Z X
XXX123
```

To translate lowercase to uppercase:

```
$ echo abc | tr [:lower:]   A-Z
ABC
$ echo abc | tr a-z A-Z
ABC
```

tr -c   --complement

'tr -c Set_1' complements (takes the opposite of) characters in Set_1. To translate any character **except** a-c and \n to '+' (Set_1 = 'a-c\n'):

```
$ echo abc123 | tr -c 'a-c\n' +
abc+++
```

To delete non-printable characters (complement of [:print:] class), except newline:

```
$ tr -cd "[:print:]\n" < a.txt
```

29: Other Related Commands - 2/2

This chapter covers a few more Unix commands related to sed. The commands in this chapter are less important than those in the previous chapter. Some readers might even skip this chapter. The GNU versions of the commands are covered.

```
tac     Print File Backwards
rev     Reverse each Line
expr    Evaluate Expression
seq     Print Number Sequence
```

tac ('cat' spelled backwards) prints a file in reverse order, last line first. For example, suppose you wanted to operate upon the last matching line in a huge file. tac would let you start from the bottom of the file, hence it would find the match much faster.

rev reverses the characters on each line. rev is not often used. But you never know when it might come in handy.

———

```
$ cat rgb
lower (#1): "red green blue"
UPPER (#2): "RED GREEN BLUE"
```

```
$ tac rgb
UPPER (#2): "RED GREEN BLUE"
lower (#1): "red green blue"
```

———

```
$ echo -e "ABC\nXYZ"
ABC
XYZ
```

```
$ echo -e "ABC\nXYZ" | rev
CBA
ZYX
```

expr - Evaluate an Expression

expr evaluates an expression and prints the result. expr can help sed do math.

Most of expr is beyond the scope of this book. We present the math operations, which are the most commonly used anyway.

Many uses of expr can be done more efficiently and easily with shell script syntax. An advantage of expr (sometimes) is that it is a separate command.

---

expr can add numbers:

```
$ expr 11 + 4
15
```

```
$ var=11
$ expr $var + 4
15
```

```
$ var=11
$ var=`expr $var + 4`
$ echo $var
15
```

Chapter 29

Note that expr requires a very specific syntax. The following variants fail to work correctly:

```
$ expr 11+4
11+4
$ expr "11 + 4"
11 + 4
```

expr can subtract numbers:

```
$ expr 11 - 4
7
```

For multiplication using expr, '*' must be protected from interpretation by the shell. Note that expr can handle negative numbers:

```
$ expr -11 \* 4
-44
```

Division with expr truncates the result to a whole number (expr only handles integers):

```
$ expr 11 / 4
2
```

The modulus operator prints the remainder from dividing two numbers:

```
$ expr 11 % 4
3
```

\(and \) can be used to force precedence, for example to evaluate '4 + 8' before '8 / 2':

```
$ expr 4 + 8 / 2
8
```

```
$ expr \( 4 + 8 \) / 2
6
```

seq - Print Number Sequence

seq prints a sequence of numbers, useful in concert with sed and other Unix utilities. There are three ways seq can be invoked:

```
seq [options] N2
seq [options] N1 N2
seq [options] N1 STEP N2
```

If single N2 argument (normally, N2 >= 1), seq prints the numbers from 1 to N2, one to a line:

```
$ seq 2
1
2
```

If two arguments, N1 and N2 (normally, N1 <= N2), seq prints the numbers from N1 to N2:

```
$ seq 98 99
98
99
```

N1 and N2 can be floating point numbers, and negative numbers are allowed:

```
$ seq -3.5 -1.5
-3.5
-2.5
-1.5
```

If three arguments (N1, STEP, N2), seq prints the numbers from N1 to N2, with an increment of STEP (0.5 in example) between each number:

```
$ seq 4.5 0.5 5.5
4.5
5.0
5.5
```

STEP can be negative, in which case the sequence is descending:

```
$ seq 8.61 -2 6
8.61
6.61
```

seq -f FMT   --format=FMT

'seq -f FMT' uses a C printf floating point format to display the numbers. Here is an example of the resulting flexibility:

```
$ seq -f "logfile%02g.txt" 3
logfile01.txt
logfile02.txt
logfile03.txt
```

seq -s STR   --separator=STR

'seq -s STR' uses STR to separate the output numbers, instead of the default \n (newline). For example, to separate numbers with '+':

```
$ seq -s '+' 5 4 34
5+9+13+17+21+25+29+33
```

As usual, combining Unix commands (such as with the bc 'basic calculator') gives you a lot of power and flexibility:

```
$ seq -s '+' 5 4 34 | bc
152
```

seq -w   --equal-width

'seq -w' makes the output numbers equal width, by padding (as needed) with leading zeroes:

```
$ seq -w 9 11
09
10
11
```

30: Definitions of Special Terms

A clearly defined vocabulary is essential in any technical field. To improve communication of sed-related concepts, this book consistently uses the following short special terms: Address, AutoPrint, BackRef, BackSlash, Cycle, Delimiter, HoldSpace, Literal, MetaChar, PatSpace, RegEx, SubEx, Word, stdin, stdout, and stderr.

Part of the confusion for learning sed is that a variety of terms are used in different books and learning resources. To help clear this up, as much as possible I have used the same terminology as the GNU sed manual. To indicate the special nature of these terms, I capitalize the ones I 'made up'.

Each special term is explained the first time it is used in the book. For your convenience, all the special terms are also defined in this chapter.

PatSpace ('Pattern Space') is the primary sed work space. Input lines, one at a time, are read into PatSpace. Most sed commands affect PatSpace. At the end of the sed script, PatSpace is (usually) 'AutoPrinted' and cleared.

HoldSpace ('Hold Space') is the secondary sed work space. A few sed commands (gG hH x) affect HoldSpace. HoldSpace is never automatically printed or cleared.

AutoPrint - At the end of a sed script, unless the -n command line option is used, sed automatically prints ('AutoPrints') PatSpace.

Cycle - In a sed 'Cycle', 1) the next input line is read into PatSpace, 2) the trailing newline is removed, 3) the sed script is run, and finally 4) sed 'AutoPrints' PatSpace (unless -n command line option).

Address - Which lines a sed command operates on. For example, in '3-6d', '3-6' is the Address (delete lines 3-6). If no Address, the command always runs.

BackRef - A 'Back Reference', such as \1, 'plays back' a previously saved \(\) expression. For example, to reverse the order of two letters, \1 and \2 play back 'x' and 'y':

```
$ echo xy | sed -r 's!(.)(.)!\2\1!'
yx
```

BackSlash - The character. In a RegEx, BackSlash converts a MetaChar to a Literal. For example, 'x*' means 0 or more 'x', but 'x' means 'x' followed by a Literal asterisk.

Definitions of Special Terms

Delimiter - The '/' character in 's/A/B/' command. You may use any visible character as the Delimiter. 's!A!B!' and 's:A:B:' are examples.

Literal - A 'Literal' is an 'ordinary' character or sequence of characters within a RegEx. For example, 'r', 'red', and '\n' are Literals. A RegEx is composed of Literals and MetaChars.

MetaChar - Each metacharacter ('MetaChar') has a special meaning within a RegEx, to do pattern matching, as explained in this book:

```
.     \w \W        *  \?  \+
\< \>    \b \B     ^  $
\( \)    \{ \}     [ ]
```

RegEx = 'Regular Expression'. RegEx is a pattern to look for, using Literals and MetaChars. 1) In 's/A/B/' command, 'A' is the RegEx. 2) In '/A/d' command, 'A' is the RegEx, used within the Address.

SubEx = 'Substitution Expression'. SubEx is a replacement pattern, using Literals and MetaChars. In 's/A/B/', 'B' is the SubEx. s replaces the first matching portion of PatSpace with SubEx.

Word - A sequence of letters, digits, and '_' characters (one or more [a-zA-Z0-9_] characters).

stdin (standard input) is the input stream for text lines going into sed. stdin typically comes from a command or file:

```
Command    $ prg | sed s/1/2/
File       $ sed s/a/b/ < if
```

stdout (standard output) is the output stream for normal sed output. stdout typically goes to the screen, another program, or a file:

```
Screen     $ sed s/a/b/ if
Program    $ sed s/a/b/ if | prg
File       $ sed s/a/b/ if > of
```

stderr (standard error) is the output stream for sed error output. stderr typically goes to the screen or a file:

```
Screen     $ sed s/a/b if
File       $ sed s/a/b if 2> ef
```

31: sed Command Line Reference

For sed command line options, there is usually a short and a long format. For example, -b is a 'short format' and --binary is a 'long format'.

The short format starts with one dash, the long format with two dashes. The two formats produce exactly the same effect. Which format you use is a personal preference.

sed -b   --binary

'sed -b' opens files in binary mode, not text mode. You will rarely if ever need to use this.

If used, it would be on Windows or Cygwin, to specify that end of line is marked with a single \n linefeed character, not preceded by a \r carriage return character. Unix does not have separate text and binary file modes, and end of line is always a single linefeed character.

sed -e script   --expression=script

'sed -e script' appends 'script' to the end of the overall sed script. The -e option is needed when more than one script is present, with a previous -e or -f option. The following two forms (-e vs ';') are equivalent:

```
$ sed -e s/1/=/ -e /RED/d rgb
lower (#=): "red green blue"
```

```
$ sed 's/1/=/; /RED/d' rgb
lower (#=): "red green blue"
```

sed -f script-file   --file=script-file

'sed -f script-file' appends the lines in script-file to the end of the overall sed script. Here is a simple -f example:

```
$ cat i2.sed
# Insert 2 lines before 'RED'
/RED/ i txt_1
/RED/ i txt_2
```

```
$ sed -e s/g/G/ -f i2.sed rgb
lower (#1): "red Green blue"
txt_1
txt_2
UPPER (#2): "RED GREEN BLUE"
```

sed --follow-symlinks

'sed --follow-symlinks' follows symbolic links when using the -i option. If -i is used with a symbolic link, you should normally also use the --follow-symlinks option.

If you run 'sed -i' on a symbolic link, and the --follow-symlinks option is **not** used, the symbolic link is converted to a regular file. This is probably not what you intended.

sed -h   --help

'sed -h' prints a summary of command line options, with somewhat similar information as this chapter. 'man sed' gives more detailed information.

Chapter 31

sed -i   --in-place

'sed -i' edits files 'in place'. Behind the scenes, sed makes a temporary file to store the intermediate results. 'sed -i' only works when input is from a file (not from stdin). Method #1 better ensures that file permissions are retained:

```
$ sed -i s/RegEx/SubEx/ a.txt
```

```
$ cp a.txt temp
$ sed s/RegEx/SubEx/ temp > a.txt
```

The -i option automatically invokes the -s option (see later). This means that -i can be used to edit several input files 'in place'.

```
$ sed -i s/A/B/ 1.txt 2.txt 3.txt
```

sed -iSuffix   --in-place=Suffix

'sed -iSuffix' edits files 'in place', with Suffix-based backup. The following two methods are equivalent:

```
$ sed -i.bak s/A/B/ log
```

```
$ cp log log.bak
$ sed -i s/A/B/ log
```

sed -l N   --line-length=N

'sed -l N' sets line-wrap length for the l (ell) command. The default is 70. A zero value tells sed not to wrap.

sed -n   --quiet   --silent

'sed -n' suppresses default AutoPrint of PatSpace when the sed script ends, and when the n command runs. Here is an example:

```
$ sed -n '$ p' rgb
UPPER (#2): "RED GREEN BLUE"
```

Because the -n flag is used, PatSpace does not AutoPrint. p prints PatSpace for the last line ($).

Note that -n option does **not** suppress other kinds of output, such as output from a, i, and c commands.

```
$ sed -n '1 a xxx' rgb
xxx
```

sed --posix

'sed --posix' disables GNU extensions to Posix sed. You will rarely if ever need to use this.

sed -r   --regexp-extended

'sed -r' uses extended regular expressions, to avoid using \ (the BackSlash) for \{, \}, \(, \), \?, \+, and \| MetaChars. For example, the two following formats are equivalent:

```
$ echo xy | sed -r "s!(.).!\1:&!"
x:xy
$ echo xy | sed "s!\(.\).!\1:&!"
x:xy
```

sed -s   --separate

Several input files are allowed on the command line. Without the -s option, the input files are considered one input stream.

With -s, the input files are considered separate files, so: 1) An Address like '/X/,/Y/' cannot span files; 2) Line numbers are reset to 1 with each file; and 3) $ refers to the last line of each file.

You will rarely if ever need to use the -s option. Note that -i automatically invokes -s, to edit one or more files 'in place'.

sed -u   --unbuffered

'sed -u' buffers input and output as little as possible. In practice, you will never need to use this. The only case where -u might be useful is:

```
$ tail -f log | sed -u -f a.sed
```

sed --version

'sed --version' prints the sed version number, and some other brief information, and then immediately exits.

sed Command Line Reference

Building the sed script - sed must have a script to run. Here are examples of how the sed script is specified:

```
$ sed s/red/xxx/ rgb
$ sed -f a.sed rgb
$ sed -e s/e/k/ -e s/:/./ rgb
$ sed 's/e/k/; s/:/./' rgb
```

The sed script is cumulative. For example, the following command appends the i2.sed script (insert lines before line containing 'RED') to the 's/g/G/' script (change g to G):

```
$ sed -e s/g/G/ -f i2.sed rgb
lower (#1): "red Green blue"
txt_1
txt_2
UPPER (#2): "RED GREEN BLUE"
```

Input from stdin - If the input file is left off the command line, or is '-', input is taken from stdin (from a pipeline or redirected from a file). So the following forms are equivalent:

```
$ echo abbc | sed s/bb/:/
a:c
```

```
$ echo abbc | sed s/bb/:/ -
a:c
```

219

32: sed Command Reference

```
Substitute          s
Delete PatSpace     dD
Append / Insert     ai
Change Text         c
Branch to Label     btT :k
Quit from sed       qQ
Access HoldSpace    hH gG x
Read Next Line      nN
Print PatSpace      pP l
Read / Write File   rR wW
Group / Comment     { } #
Other Actions       evyz =
```

```
Multi-Line Ops     GH N DPW s
GNU Extensions     evz QT RW
Ends Script        c dD qQ
```

Command Addresses

sed commands take an optional Address. 'd' (no Address) runs on all lines, '4 d' on line #4, '1,2 d' on lines 1-2, '/zz/ d' if PatSpace contains 'zz'. Full syntax for a few example commands is:

```
[a1,[a2]] b k
[a1,[a2]] a Txt
[a1,[a2]] d
[a1,[a2]] r Rfile
```

q and Q just take ONE Address, in contrast to other sed commands, which can take two. For example, '9 q' quits on line #9, and '/zz/ q' quits if PatSpace contains 'zz'.

Substitute: s

```
s/RegEx/SubEx/[flags]
```

's/RegEx/SubEx/[flags]' searches for RegEx in PatSpace, and replaces ('substitutes') one or more matching portions of PatSpace with SubEx. The s command 'finds and replaces'.

The [flags] are optional. Each flag, if included, turns on a particular setting.

MetaChars (for RegEx and SubEx) give great flexibility for finding and replacing. See Chapters 4-9 for full information on MetaChars.

```
[ ] .   \w \W    * \? \+
\< \> \b \B    \( \)    \{ \}
& \l \u \L \U \E    \1 \2 ...
```

Delete PatSpace: dD

```
d
```

d ('delete') deletes PatSpace, ends the sed script, reads the next input line into PatSpace, and restarts the script.

```
D
```

If no \n (newline) in PatSpace, D ('Delete') behaves the same as the d command. If \n **is** in PatSpace, D deletes PatSpace line #1, including the first \n, and restarts the sed script **without** reading the next line.

Chapter 32

Append / Insert / Change: aic

```
a Txt
```

'a Txt' ('append') schedules 'Txt' for later output. 'Txt' is written to standard output, either 1) just before N or n command tries to get the next input line, or 2) at the end of the sed script (after any AutoPrint).

'a Txt' does **not** change PatSpace. Appended text cannot be edited by subsequent script commands.

```
i Txt
```

'i Txt' ('insert') immediately inserts 'Txt' before the current line. The inserted text cannot be changed by subsequent script commands.

```
c Txt
```

'c Txt' ('change') deletes PatSpace, skips the rest of the sed script, prints 'Txt', and then restarts a Cycle by reading the next input line.

Branch to Label: btT :k

```
:Label
```

A 'Label' is the destination for b, t, or T. So ':k' is the destination for 'b k' (or 'bk'). For one-line, simple scripts, keep Labels short.

:f, :j, :k, and :loop are four examples of typical Labels (using a letter not otherwise used in sed, or a short word).

```
b [Label]
```

b ('branch') branches to end of the sed script.
bk (or 'b k') branches to the :k Label.

```
   t [Label]
```

t ('test') branches to the end of the sed script if s replaced since the current line was read, or since the last t/T branch was taken.

tk (or 't k') applies the same test, but branches to the :k Label.

```
   T [Label]
```

T ('Test') branches to the end of the sed script if s has **not** replaced since the current line was read, or since the last t/T branch was taken.

Tk (or 'T k') applies the same test, but branches to the :k Label.

Quit from sed: qQ

```
   q [exit-code]
```

q ('quit') quits sed without processing more commands or input. PatSpace is printed (unless -n command line option). q takes a single Address, such as '9q', and an optional exit code, such as 'q3'.

```
   Q [exit-code]
```

Q ('Quit') quits sed without processing more commands or input. PatSpace is **not** printed. Q takes a single Address, such as '9Q', and an optional exit code, such as 'Q1'. Q is a GNU extension.

Access HoldSpace: hH gG x

```
   h
```

h ('hold') copies the contents of PatSpace to HoldSpace. The original contents of HoldSpace are overwritten.

Chapter 32

```
                    H
```

H ('Hold') **appends** the contents of PatSpace to HoldSpace, after a newline character. The original contents of HoldSpace are retained.

```
                    g
```

g ('get') copies the contents of HoldSpace to PatSpace. The original contents of PatSpace are overwritten.

```
                    G
```

G ('Get') **appends** the contents of HoldSpace to PatSpace, after a newline character. The original contents of PatSpace are retained.

```
                    x
```

x ('exchange') swaps the contents of PatSpace and HoldSpace. Any previous contents of PatSpace and HoldSpace are overwritten.

Read Next Line: nN

```
                    n
```

n ('next') reads the next input line into PatSpace. n prints PatSpace before trying to read the line, unless the -n command line option is used.

The sed script normally continues after n runs. But if no more input for n to read, sed exits, without trying to print PatSpace again.

```
                    N
```

sed Command Reference

N ('Next') appends the next input line to PatSpace, after a newline. The sed script normally continues after N runs. But if no more input for N to read, sed exits, after printing PatSpace (if -n command line option not used).

Print PatSpace: pP l

```
p
```

p ('print') prints PatSpace to the output stream.

```
P
```

P ('Print') prints PatSpace line #1, up to the first \n (newline). If no \n, P behaves the same as p (prints entire PatSpace).

```
l [line-wrap]
```

l ('list') displays PatSpace in a special format, such as '1\n2$', for debugging. l is not typically used for production scripts.

l takes an optional line-wrap parameter. 'l 70' (default unless changed by -l command line option) splits long lines at 70 characters. 'l 0' turns off line-wrap.

Read / Write File: rR wW

```
r Rfile
```

'r Rfile' ('read') schedules printing Rfile contents, either 1) just before N or n command tries to get the next input line, or 2) at the end of the sed script (after sed AutoPrints).

If Rfile cannot be read, r does nothing, and no error occurs. If Rfile is /dev/stdin, input is taken from standard input.

```
R Rfile
```

'R Rfile' ('Read') schedules printing the next line from Rfile, either 1) just before N or n command tries to get the next input line, or 2) at the end of the sed script (after sed AutoPrints).

Each R invocation reads the next line from Rfile. The first time, line #1 is read, the second time, line #2, etc.

If Rfile cannot be read, or is at end of file, R does nothing, and no error occurs. If Rfile is /dev/stdin, input is taken from standard input.

```
w Wfile
```

'w Wfile' ('write') appends PatSpace to Wfile. Wfile is created (or truncated) at sed startup. If Wfile cannot be written, sed exits with an error. Wfile is kept open until sed exits.

- 'w /dev/stdout' writes PatSpace to stdout.
- 'w /dev/stderr' writes PatSpace to stderr.

```
W Wfile
```

'W Wfile' ('Write') appends line #1 of PatSpace (up to any first newline) to Wfile. W is a GNU extension.

Wfile is created (or truncated) at sed startup. If Wfile cannot be written, sed exits with an error. Wfile is kept open until sed exits.

- 'W /dev/stdout' writes line #1 to stdout.
- 'W /dev/stderr' writes line #2 to stderr.

Group Commands: { }

```
{ }
```

{ } ('group') defines a command group. If the Address for the group matches, commands in the group are run.

You may nest { } within another { } group. Also, a command within { } may use its own Address.

There is no point in using { } without an Address. A group only influences sed script behavior if the group has an Address.

Comment:

```
# Example Comment
```

All text after the # symbol, up to the end of the line, is a comment. This is useful for documenting sed scripts.

As a special case, #n at top of a sed script has the same effect as the -n command line option.

Other Actions: evyz =

```
e [command]
```

e ('execute' or 'evaluate') executes the command in PatSpace, and replaces PatSpace with the output (minus the trailing newline).

'e command' executes 'command', and immediately prints any output to the output stream.

```
v [required-version]
```

v ('version') does nothing. v is related to script portability. Other versions of sed, that do **not** have the v command, fail when they encounter v.

Also, v takes an optional argument (default = 4.0) to specify the version of GNU sed the script requires. You will probably never use v.

```
y/src/dst/
```

y ('transliterate') transliterates source characters to destination characters. For example, 'y/ab/AB/' changes 'a' to 'A', 'b' to 'B'.

```
z
```

z ('zap') clears PatSpace. z is usually the same as 's/.*//'. However, 's/.*//' will fail if there are invalid multi-byte sequences in the input stream.

Chapter 32

```
=
```

= ('line #') prints the line number for one or more lines, followed by a new-line. The = command is not used much in sed scripts.

Multi-Line Ops: GH N DPW s

The following sed commands can do multi-line operations:
G ('Get') appends HoldSpace to PatSpace. H ('Hold') appends PatSpace to HoldSpace.
N ('Next') appends the next input line to PatSpace.
D ('Delete') deletes PatSpace line #1; P ('Print') prints it; 'W Wfile' ('Write') writes it to Wfile.
In addition, s ('substitute') can edit a multi-line PatSpace.

GNU Extensions: evz QT RW

e ('execute'), v ('version'), z ('zap'), Q ('Quit'), T ('Test'), 'R Rfile' ('Read'), and 'W Wfile' ('Write') are GNU extensions. In addition, some command options are GNU extensions, for example the e ('execute') and m ('multi-line') flags to the s command.

Ends Script: c dD qQ

The following sed commands always skip to the end of the sed script:
'c Txt' ('change') deletes PatSpace, skips the rest of the sed script, prints 'Txt', and then restarts a Cycle by reading the next input line.

d ('delete') deletes PatSpace, ends the sed script, reads the next input line into PatSpace, and restarts the script.

If no \n (newline) in PatSpace, D ('Delete') behaves the same as the d command. If \n **is** in PatSpace, D deletes PatSpace line #1, including the first \n, and restarts the sed script **without** reading the next line.

q ('quit') and Q ('Quit') stop processing the sed script (the script is aborted), and also stop reading input (exit sed).

n ('next') and N ('Next') also skip to the end of the sed script, but only if no more input. And of course b ('branch'), t ('test'), and T ('Test') can skip to the end of the sed script.

33: s Command Flag Reference

```
i   Ignore case when matching
g   Global substitution on line
n   Number of match to change
p   Print the result if match
w   Write result to file if match
e   Execute PatSpace to PatSpace
m   Multi-Line Mode Matching
```

```
g n    Sets Match to Change
p w    Prints / Writes Output
  w    Must be the Last Flag
e m    Is a GNU Extension
```

i Flag: Ignore Case

The i (ignore case) flag for the s command tells sed to ignore uppercase vs lowercase when looking for a match in PatSpace. The flag can be 'i' or 'I' (capital eye). 'i' is preferred.

```
$ echo old | sed s/Old/123/
old
```

```
$ echo old | sed s/Old/123/i
123
```

229

Chapter 33

g Flag: Global

The g (global) flag for the s command tells sed to change **all** matches, not just the first match.

```
$ echo aaaaa | sed s/a/X/
Xaaaa
$ echo aaaaa | sed s/a/X/g
XXXXX
```

n Flag: Number

The n (number) flag for the s command tells sed to change one specified match, instead of match #1. A number, such as 2 or 3, is substituted for n.

```
$ echo aaaaa | sed s/a/=/
=aaaa
$ echo aaaaa | sed s/a/=/3
aa=aa
```

p Flag: Print

The p (print) flag for the s command prints PatSpace to stdout, after replacement, **if** a replacement was done.

```
$ sed -n 's/red/123/p' rgb
lower (#1): "123 green blue"
```

w Flag: Write

The w (write) flag for the s command writes PatSpace to a file, after replacement, **if** a replacement was done.

```
$ sed -n 's/red/123/w a.txt' rgb
$ cat a.txt
lower (#1): "123 green blue"
```

e Flag: Execute

The e (execute) flag for the s command executes PatSpace as a command, **if** a substitution was made. The command output is copied back into PatSpace.

```
$ echo 2 | sed 's/./expr & + 4/e'
6
```

m Flag: Multi-line

The m (multi-line) flag for the s command triggers 'multi-line mode': ^ also matches the empty string after a newline, and $ also matches the empty string before a newline.

```
$ seq 2 | sed 'N; s/^2/=/'
1
2
```

```
$ seq 2 | sed 'N; s/^2/=/m'
1
=
```

Chapter 33

Combining Flags

Any flag for the s command may be combined with any other flag, with a few special cases:

1) The w flag **must** come last, followed by a file name. For example, 'w' comes after 'g' in 's/old/new/gw a.txt'.

2) Do **not** use the same flag more than once. For example, 's/A/B/gg' produces an error message.

3) Combining n and g tells sed to change match occurrences n, n+1, n+2, etc.

```
$ sed 's/[aeiou]/=/3g' rgb
lower (#1): "r=d gr==n bl=="
UPPER (#2): "RED GREEN BLUE"
```

34: Address and RegEx Reference

Each sed command takes an optional Address. The Address determines whether to run the command. Here are some Address examples:

```
    2 d         /[a-z]99/ d
    $ d            /[13]/ d
    $!d            /Ford/ d
  1,6 d        /Ford/,+22 d
  1~2 d         /aa/,/bb/ d
  3,$ d         /aa/,/bb/! d
  1,6! d         /xyz/,~5 d
  1~2! d          2,/xyz/ d
```

Address Omitted

If no Address, the command always runs.

```
$ seq 4 | sed 'd'
```

N Format Address

An 'N Format' Address runs the sed command on line N. A value of $ for N means 'last line'.

```
$ seq 4 | sed '1 d'
2
3
4
```

Chapter 34

L,H Format Address

An 'L,H' Address (low, high) runs the sed command on lines L to H, inclusive. H can be $ (last line). If L > H (not advisable), then only line L matches.

```
$ seq 8 | sed '1,6 d'
7
8
```

/RegEx/ Format Address

A '/RegEx/' Address runs the sed command on lines where PatSpace contains RegEx. The '_RegEx_' syntax can be used to avoid use of '/'. The format '/RegEx/I' (capital eye) is case-insensitive.

```
$ sed '/red/ d' rgb
UPPER (#2): "RED GREEN BLUE"
```

/RegEx/,/RegEx/ Address

'/b/,/g/' runs the sed command over a range, starting with the first line containing 'b', and ending with the first line containing 'g'.
If 'g' never matches, all lines starting with the first matching line match. '/b/,/g/' can specify more than one range, if the range recurs.

```
$ sed '/b/,/g/ d' a-i.txt
a
h
i
```

Address and RegEx Reference

L,/RegEx/ Format Address

'L,/RegEx/' runs the command for a range of lines, starting at line L (Low), and ending at the next line where RegEx matches part of PatSpace.

If RegEx never matches, all lines starting with line L match. If line #1 contains RegEx, '0,/RE/' (a GNU extension) makes line #1 the end of the range.

```
$ sed '1,/g/ d' a-i.txt
h
i
```

/RegEx/,+N Format Address

A '/RegEx/,+N' Address runs the sed command if PatSpace contains RegEx, plus runs the sed command on the next N lines.

```
$ sed '/b/,+5 d' a-i.txt
a
h
i
```

/RegEx/,~N Format Address

A '/RegEx/,~N' Address runs the sed command if PatSpace contains RegEx, and also runs the sed command on lines up to the next line that is a multiple of N.

```
$ sed '/b/,~8 d' a-i.txt
a
i
```

Chapter 34

First~Step Address

A 'First~Step' Address runs the sed command on the 'First' line, the 'First + Step' line, the 'First + Step + Step' line, etc. So '1~2' matches 1, 3, 5, etc.

```
$ seq 5 | sed '1~2 d'
2
4
```

! (Inverts Address Match)

A '!' directly after the Address inverts the sense of matching.

```
   3!    Is not line #3
   $!    Is not last line
 1,2!    Is not line 1-2
 /ZZ/!   ZZ not in PatSpace
```

```
$ seq 4 | sed '$!  d'
4
```

RegEx = 'Regular Expression'. RegEx is a pattern to look for, using Literals and MetaChars. 1) In 's/A/B/' command, 'A' is the RegEx. 2) In '/A/d' command, 'A' is the RegEx, used within the Address.

Literal Characters

```
         Matches
 an      'an' in mantis
 man     'man' in mantis
 ant     'ant' in mantis
```

BackSlash Literal Characters

```
        Matches
\.      '.' in 3.14159
\*      '*' in 3 * 3 = 9
\\      '\' in c:\windows\
```

```
\a  Alert (ASCII 7)
\n  Newline (ASCII 10)
\f  Form Feed (ASCII 12)
\r  Carriage Return (ASCII 13)
\t  Horizontal Tab (ASCII 9)
\v  Vertical Tab (ASCII 11)
```

```
\d010  Decimal 010 (ASCII 10)
\o012  Octal 012 (ASCII 10)
\x0A   Hex 0A (ASCII 10)
```

Word Boundary MetaChars

```
                 Is Match
\<an or \ban     'an' in antic
an\> or an\b     'an' in span
```

```
                 NOT Match
\<an or \ban     'an' in span
an\> or an\b     'an' in antic
```

Chapter 34

```
            Is Match
   \Ban    'an' in span
   an\B    'an' in antic
```

```
            NOT Match
   \Ban    'an' in antic
   an\B    'an' in span
```

'Word' is a sequence of [a-zA-Z0-9_] characters.

Line Boundary MetaChars

```
           Only Matches
   ^The    'The' at start of line
   End$    'End' at end of line
```

Wildcard MetaChars

```
         Matches
   \w    Word character (eg, bB2_)
   \W    Non-Word (eg, #$%&+=><)
   .     Any (Word or Non-Word)
```

[Character Set] MetaChars

```
                 Matches
   [a-cz]         a, b, c, or z
   [^a-cz]    NOT a, b, c, or z
   []^a-c-]      ], ^, a, b, c, or -
```

238

Posix Character Classes

```
      Equivalent Expressions
[[:lower:]]   [a-z] (English)
[[:upper:]]   [A-Z]
[[:digit:]]   [0-9]
[[:alpha:]]   [a-zA-Z]
[[:alnum:]]   [a-zA-Z0-9]
[[:xdigit:]]  [a-fA-F0-9]
```

```
      Equivalent Expressions
[[:blank:]]   [ \t]
[[:space:]]   [ \t\r\n\v\f]
[[:graph:]]   [\x21-\x7E]
[[:print:]]   [\x20-\x7E]
[[:cntrl:]]   [\x00-\x1F\x7F]
[[:punct:]]   See Chapter 4
```

Simple Repetition MetaChars

```
        Matches
9*      0-any 9 ('', '9', ...)
9\+     1-any 9 ('9', '99', ...)
9\?     0-1 9's ('' or '9')
9+ 9?   Syntax with -r option
```

```
        Matches
.*      0-any of any character
.\+     1-any of any character
.\?     0-1 of any character
.+ .?   Syntax with -r option
```

```
           Matches
\(ha\)*    0-any ha ('', ha, ...)
\(ha\)\+   1-any ha (ha, haha, ...)
\(ha\)\?   0-1 ha ('' or ha)
(ha)?      Syntax with -r option
```

General Repetition MetaChars

```
           Matches
9\{8\}     Exactly 8 (99999999)
9\{0,2\}   0, 1, or 2 ('', 9, 99)
9\{2,\}    2-any (99, 999, ...)
9{2,}      Syntax with -r option
```

Other MetaChars

```
\|         Alternative Patterns
\( \)      Grouping and Saving
\`         Always Start of PatSpace
\'         Always End of PatSpace
```

SubEx = 'Substitution Expression'. SubEx is a replacement pattern, using Literals and MetaChars. In 's/A/B/', 'B' is the SubEx. s replaces the first matching portion of PatSpace with SubEx.

& (Entire Matched Portion)

In a SubEx, '&' substitutes (inserts) the entire matched portion of PatSpace.

```
$ seq 3 | sed 's/./Line &/'
Line 1
Line 2
Line 3
```

\N BackRef (Play Saved Group)

A 'Back Reference', such as \1, 'plays back' a previously saved \(\) expression. For example, to reverse the order of two letters, \1 and \2 play back 'x' and 'y':

```
$ echo xy | sed -r 's!(.)(.)!\2\1!'
yx
```

\l \u (Case for Next Character)

In a SubEx, '\l' changes the next character to lowercase; '\u' changes the next character to uppercase.

```
$ sed 's/r../\u&/g' rgb
loweR (#1): "Red gReen blue"
UPPER (#2): "RED GREEN BLUE"
```

\L \U \E (Case for Next Span)

In a SubEx, '\L' changes the rest of SubEx to lowercase, until the next '\U' or '\E'. '\U' changes the rest of SubEx to uppercase, until the next '\L' or '\E'.

```
$ sed 's/g../\U&/g' rgb
lower (#1): "red GREen blue"
UPPER (#2): "RED GREEN BLUE"
```

35: Related Books and Web Sites

The following books and web sites have useful information concerning sed, regular expressions, and shell scripting.

Books:

Advanced Bash Scripting Guide (2010)
Mendel Cooper / lulu.com
ISBN: 978-1435752184

GNU Bash Reference Manual (2003)
Chet Ramey and Brian Fox
Network Theory
ISBN: 978-0954161774

Learning the bash Shell (2005)
Cameron Newham
O'Reilly Media
ISBN: 978-0596009656

Linux in a Nutshell (2009)
Ellen Siever and other Authors
O'Reilly Media
ISBN: 978-0596154486

Mastering Regular Expressions (2006)
Jeffery Friedl / O'Reilly Media
ISBN: 978-0596528126

Mastering Shell Scripting (2008)
Randal Michael / Wiley
ISBN: 978-0470183014

sed & awk (1997)
Dale Dougherty and Arnold Robbins
O'Reilly Media
ISBN: 1565922255

Unix Power Tools (2002)
Shelly Powers and other Authors
O'Reilly Media
ISBN: 978-0596003302

Unix Shell Programming (2003)
Stephen Kochan and Patrick Wood
SAMS Publishing
ISBN: 978-0672324901

Web Sites:

Aurelio Jargas
"sed $HOME" (2011)
http://sed.sourceforge.net/

Aurelio Jargas
sedsed - Debug SED scripts (2004)
http://aurelio.net/sedsed/

Bruce Barnett
"sed - An Introduction and Tutorial" (2011)
http://www.grymoire.com/Unix/

Chet Ramey
"Bash Reference Manual" (2010)
http://www.gnu.org/software/bash/manual/bashref.html

Daniel Robbins
"sed by Example" (2000)
http://www.ibm.com/developerworks/1/library/l-sed1/index.html

Daniel Robbins, modifed by Gentoo staff
"sed by Example" (2010)
http://www.gentoo.org/doc/en/articles/l-sed1.xml

Eric Pement
Useful One-Line Scripts for SED (2005)
http://sed.sourceforge.net/sed1line.txt

Eric Pement
"sed ... the stream editor" (2011)
http://www.pement.org/sed/

Chapter 35

Eric Pement
The SED FAQ (2003)
http://sed.sourceforge.net/sedfaq.html

Karl Syring
UnxUtils (2011) - Win32 Unix Utilities
http://unxutils.sourceforge.net/

Lee E. McMahon
"SED -- A Non-interactive Text Editor" (1978)
http://sed.sourceforge.net/grabbag/tutorials/sed_mcmahon.txt

Paolo Bonzini
"sed, a Stream Editor" (GNU manual) (2004)
http://www.gnu.org/software/sed/manual/sed.html

Paolo Bonzini
"seder's grab bag" (2006)
http://sed.sourceforge.net/grabbag/

Peteris Krumins
"Famous Sed One-Liners Explained" (2010)
http://www.catonmat.net/blog/sed-one-liners-explained-part-one/

Sven Guckes
"sed-users" Yahoo Group (ongoing)
http://groups.yahoo.com/group/sed-users/

Yao-Jen Chang
SED & Regular Expressions (2012)
http://www.rtfiber.com.tw/~changyj/sed/

Concepts Index

-e Command Line Option for sed, 12, 214
-f Command Line Option for sed, 14, 215
-i Command Line Option for sed, 20, 216
-n Command Line Option for sed, 22, 217
-r Command Line Option for sed, 53, 218

Accessing HoldSpace, 112
Addresses for sed Commands, 73, 212
Alternatives to sed (awk, perl), 2
Anchor Metacharacters, 42, 237
AutoPrint when sed Script Ends, 3, 22, 212

BackRef (Back Reference), 68, 212, 241
BackSlash ('\'), 10, 212
BackSlash Best Avoided, 10

Cannot Edit a, i, c Results, 95
Combining s Command Flags, 27
Comparison of * \+ \? , 56
Cycle (Starts by Reading Line), 3, 212
Cycle Explained with an Example, 4

Definitions of Special Terms, xv, 212
Delimiter Alternatives, 10
Delimiter for s Command, 9, 213

ed, the Precursor to sed, 2
expr (Evaluate an Expression), 207
Extended Regular Expressions, 53, 218

Flags for s (substitute) Command, 19, 229
Flags for sed s Command, 19

General Advice about using sed, 127
General Repetition Metacharacters, 58, 240
GNU sed Advantages, xiii, xiv
Greedy Pattern Matching, 52, 55, 59
grep (Print Matching Lines), 182

head (Print First Part of File), 195
History of sed, 2
HoldSpace (Secondary sed Buffer), 3, 212

Chapter 35

Input to sed from File or stdin, 11
Inputs used in Book Examples, 6
Installing sed, xiv
Introducing the s Command, 4

Leaning Toothpick Style best Avoided, 10
Limiting the Extent of a Matching Segment, 52, 53
Line Orientation of sed, 2, 16
Literal Characters, 29, 213

MetaChars (Metacharacters), 32, 213

Output from sed to File or stdout, 15

PatSpace (Primary sed Buffer), 3, 212
Posix Character Classes, 38, 239
Prerequisites to Learning sed, xv
Preventing Mistakes when using sed, 18, 131

Quoting Command-Line Scripts, 5, 128

RegEx (Regular Expression), 4, 213
Related Books and Web Sites, 242
rev (Reverse each Line), 206

sed Command Line Options, 12, 214
sed Command Reference, 220
sed Contrasted with vi, 1
sed Line Counter, 3, 109
sedsed Testing Utility, 100
seq (Print Sequence of Numbers), 7, 209
Simple Repetition Metacharacters, 50, 239, 240
Single Character Metacharacters, 29
Special Terms related to sed, xv, 212
Structuring Input Files, 131
SubEx (Substitution Expression), 4, 213
stderr (standard error), 213
stdin (standard input), 11, 213
stdout (standard output), 10, 213

tac (Print File in Reverse Order), 206
tail (Print Last Part of File), 197
Testing sed Scripts, 131
tr (Translate Characters), 203

uniq (Handle Adjacent Repeated Lines), 200
Unix Command Prompt, 2
Unix echo Command, 7
Unix Philosophy, 1
Unix Pipe for Connecting Commands, 2
UnxUtils for Windows, xv, 6

Concepts Index

Using sed within Shell Scripts, 130

Versions of sed, xiv

What is a sed Script?, 5
What is sed?, 1
When to Use (or not Use) sed, 127
Word (as Used by sed), 37, 213

; to Separate sed Script Commands, 13

Command / Syntax Index

Addresses for sed Commands
    Address Omitted, 74, 233
    N Format Address, 74, 233
    L,H Format Address, 75, 234
    /RegEx/ Format Address, 76, 234
    /RegEx/,/RegEx/ Address, 78, 234
    L,/RegEx/ Format Address, 79, 235
    /RegEx/,+N Format Address, 81, 235
    /RegEx/,~N Format Address, 82, 235
    First~Step Address, 83, 236
    ! (Inverts Address Match), 84, 236

Flags for sed s Command
    e (execute), 25, 231
    g (global), 21, 230
    i (ignore case), 20, 229
    m (multi), 26, 231
    n (number), 21, 230
    p (print), 23, 230
    combining flags, 232

grep Command Line Options
    grep --help, 188
    grep -b --byte-offset, 184
    grep -c --count, 184
    grep -e PAT --regexp=PAT, 185
    grep -E --extended-regexp, 185
    grep -f FILE --file=FILE, 186
    grep -F --fixed-strings, 186
    grep -h --no-filename, 187
    grep -H --with-filename, 187
    grep -i --ignore-case, 188
    grep -l --files-with-matches, 188
    grep -L --files-without-matches, 189
    grep -m N --max-count=N, 189
    grep -n --line-number, 189
    grep -o --only-matching, 190
    grep -q --quiet --silent, 190
    grep -r -R --recursive, 191
    grep -u --unix-byte-offsets, 191
    grep -v --invert-match, 191

Command / Syntax Index

grep -w   --word-regexp, 192
grep -x   --line-regexp, 192
grep -A N   --after-context=N, 192
grep -B N   --before-context=N, 193
grep -C N   --context=N, 194

head Command Line Options
    head -c -N   --bytes=-N, 196
    head -c N   --bytes=N, 196
    head -n -N   --lines=-N, 196
    head -n N   --lines=N, 195
    head -q   --quiet   --silent, 197
    head -v   --verbose, 197

Metacharacters: Anchoring
    ^ (Start of PatSpace), 42, 238
    $ (End of PatSpace), 44, 238
    \<   \>   \b (Word Boundaries), 46, 237
    \B (Not a Word Boundary), 49, 238

Metacharacters: General Repetition
    \{N\} (Exact N of Previous), 58, 240
    \{L,\} (Low, Higher of Previous), 59, 240
    \{L,H\} (Low, High of Previous), 60, 240

Metacharacters: Simple Repetition
    * (0 or More of Previous), 50, 239
    \+ (1 or More of Previous), 53, 239
    \? (0 or 1 of Previous), 54, 239
    *   \+   \? Compared, 56

Metacharacters: Single Characters
    Literal Character, 29, 236
    . (Any Character), 32, 238
    Specify Literal Character, 32, 237
    [ ] Character Set, 34, 238
    \w (Word), 36, 238
    \W (Non-Word), 36, 238
    [: :] (Posix class), 38, 239

Metacharacters: Unclassified
    \| (Alternative Patterns), 62, 240
    \(\) (Grouping and Saving), 63, 240
    \` (Always Start of PatSpace), 65, 240
    \' (Always End of PatSpace), 65, 240

Metacharacters: Substitution Expression
    & (Entire Matched Portion), 67, 240
    \N BackRef (Play Saved Group), 68, 212, 241
    \l   \u (Case for Next Character), 70, 241

Chapter 35

\L \U \E (Case for Next Span), 71, 241

sed Command Line Options
- sed --follow-symlinks, 215
- sed --posix, 217
- sed --version, 218
- sed -b --binary, 214
- sed -e script --expression=script, 12, 214
- sed -f script-file --file=script-file, 14, 215
- sed -h --help, 215
- sed -iSuffix --in-place=Suffix, 216
- sed -i --in-place, 17, 216
- sed -l N --line-length=N, 217
- sed -n --quiet --silent, 22, 217
- sed -r --regexp-extended, 53, 218
- sed -s --separate, 218
- sed -u --unbuffered, 218

sed Commands
- sed : (Label, eg :k), 116, 222
- sed = Command (line #), 125, 228
- sed # (comment marker), 123, 227
- sed { } (grouping), 121, 226
- sed a Command (append), 90, 222
- sed b Command (branch), 116, 222
- sed c Command (change), 92, 222
- sed D Command (Delete), 89, 221
- sed d Command (delete), 86, 221
- sed e Command (execute), 124, 227
- sed G Command (Get), 113, 224
- sed g Command (get), 113, 224
- sed H Command (Hold), 113, 224
- sed h Command (hold), 113, 223
- sed i Command (insert), 91, 222
- sed l Command (display line), 100, 225
- sed N Command (Next Line), 111, 225
- sed n Command (next line), 109, 224
- sed P Command (Print), 99, 225
- sed p Command (print), 98, 225
- sed Q Command (Quit), 120, 223
- sed q Command (quit), 119, 223
- sed R Command (Read Rfile), 103, 226
- sed r Command (read Rfile), 102, 225
- sed s Command (substitute), 9, 221
- sed T Command (Test), 117, 223
- sed t Command (test), 117, 223
- sed v Command (version), 124, 227
- sed W Command (Write Wfile), 107, 226
- sed w Command (write Wfile), 105, 226

Command / Syntax Index

sed x Command (exchange), 113, 224
sed y Command (transliterate), 124, 227
sed z Command (zap), 125, 227

seq Command Line Options
    seq -f FMT --format=FMT, 210
    seq -s STR --separator=STR, 211
    seq -w --equal-width, 211

tail Command Line Options
    tail -c +N --bytes=+N, 198
    tail -c N --bytes=N, 198
    tail -f --follow, 199
    tail -n +N --lines=+N, 198
    tail -n N --lines=N, 197
    tail -q --quiet --silent, 199
    tail -s N --sleep-interval=N, 199
    tail -v --verbose, 199

tr Command Line Options
    tr -c --complement, 205
    tr -d --delete, 204
    tr -s --squeeze-repeats, 204

uniq Command Line Options
    uniq -c --count, 200
    uniq -d --repeated, 200
    uniq -f N --skip-fields=N, 201
    uniq -i --ignore-case, 201
    uniq -s N --skip-chars=N, 202
    uniq -u --unique, 202
    uniq -w N --check-chars=N, 202

Script Examples Index

Examples - Branching Commands, 117

Examples - HoldSpace Commands, 114

Examples - Substitution
    Add Leader at Line Start, 135
    Delete Space at Line End, 135
    Delete Space at Line Start, 135
    Do a Simple Substitution, 134
    Replace All or Just One, 137
    Replace with Entire Match, 137
    Substitute for a Span, 134
    Substitute for One or More (+), 136
    Substitute on Certain Lines, 137
    Substitute only for a Word, 136
    Substitute up to Something, 136

Examples - Line Spacing
    Double Space a Stream, 138
    Squeeze Blank Lines to One, 140
    Triple Space a Stream, 139

Examples - Add Some Lines
    Add Line After Lines 2, 3, ..., 142
    Add Line After Matching Line, 144
    Add Line Before Lines 1, 3, ..., 142
    Add Line Before Matching Line, 143
    Add Line Before & After Line, 145

Examples - Delete Some Lines
    Delete All Blank Lines, 155
    Delete First X Lines, 153
    Delete Following Matched Line, 157
    Delete Last Line, 153
    Delete Last X Lines, 154
    Delete Leading Blank Lines, 156
    Delete Line #X, 152
    Delete Lines 1, 3, ..., 154
    Delete Lines L to H, 153
    Delete Match-Based Range, 157
    Delete Serial Duplicate Lines, 158
    Delete Up to Blank Line #1, 156

Script Examples Index

Examples - Print Some Lines
    Number Lines in Stream, 151
    Print First X Lines, 147
    Print Last Line, 146
    Print Last X Lines, 148
    Print Line #X, 146
    Print Line After Match, 150
    Print Line Before Match, 149
    Print Lines 4, 8, ..., 149
    Print Lines L to H, 147
    Print Matching Line, 149

Examples - Other Short Tasks
    Add Commas to Numbers, 165
    Capitalize Words, 161
    Count Lines in Stream, 160
    Delete Duplicate Characters, 161
    Format a Phone Number, 161
    Replace First Match in File, 162
    Reverse Each Line, 163
    Reverse Each Word, 162
    Reverse Order of Lines, 164

Examples - Complex Tasks
    Add Headers and Footers, 166
    Delete HTML Tags, 178
    Multi-Line Find and Replace, 170
    Set Incremental Macro Values, 174

Made in the USA
Lexington, KY
31 October 2013